SOURCE BOOKS ON EDUCATION
VOL. 41

TEACHING ENGLISH AS A SECOND LANGUAGE

GARLAND REFERENCE LIBRARY
OF SOCIAL SCIENCE
VOL. 750

TEACHING ENGLISH AS A SECOND LANGUAGE

A Resource Guide

Angela L. Carrasquillo

GARLAND PUBLISHING, Inc.
New York & London / 1994

Library of Congress Cataloging-in-Publication Data

Carrasquillo, Angela.
  Teaching English as a second language : a resource
guide / by Angela L. Carrasquillo.
    p.   cm. — (Garland reference library of social
science ; vol. 750. Source books on education ; vol. 41)
  Includes indexes.
  ISBN 0–8153–0821–3
  1. English language—Study and teaching—Foreign
speakers—Bibliography.   I. Title.   II. Series: Garland
reference library of social science ; vol. 750.   III. Series:
Garland reference library of social science. Source books
on education vol. 41.
  Z5818.E5C37   1994
  [PE1128.A2]
  016.428'007—dc20   93–41180
                                                   CIP

Printed on acid-free, 250-year-life paper
Manufactured in the United States of America

Contents

Preface

This book combines theory and research with practical classroom applications, encompassing both general theoretical guidelines and specific teaching techniques. It was written for English as a second language educators, especially teachers and prospective teachers who work with limited English proficient students of all language backgrounds. It provides a holistic picture of the many dimensions in teaching English to individuals for whom English is not their primary language. Another objective of the book is to bring together new discoveries in the language classroom, new insights from research, and new trends in educational policies contributing to new directions in second language learning and teaching. The content is drawn on the insights offered by the major disciplines of psychology, linguistics, anthropology, sociology, and direct observations of limited English proficient students and ESL teachers in diverse settings. These new theories are presented in a simplified way to help ESL educators understand the theoretical foundations on which practical applications are based. This is one of the reasons why the language of the text is simple, easy to read and understand; and the complex linguistic concepts, citations and quotations are reduced to the minimum in order for the reader to concentrate on the meaning and interpretation of the information provided as it relates to the second language classroom situation.

English as a second language often involves a link between language, ethnicity and culture, and it is manifested by diversified curricular goals and teaching patterns in the classroom. Throughout the book, the author emphasizes that language and culture are integral components of the instructional process in ESL classrooms, and as such, they are important foundations upon which cognitive and affective development are based. Emphasis is placed on building on the strengths that language minority individuals bring to the target language rather than identifying deficits to be corrected. The role of the students' linguistic, cognitive, and academic development in their native language as well as students' own desire to learn in English are important variables in learning and teaching a second language.

The book is organized into 12 chapters:

Chapter 1: Linguistic Foundations. It provides an overview of the linguistic support on which second language acquisition and second language learning are established, including definitions of second language acquisition, English as a second language, the nature of language in children, and language in adolescence and beyond. It includes an overview of trends in second language theory.

Chapter 2: Second Language Learners. The chapter identifies and discusses special characteristics of students in ESL classes, including individual differences, and language and literacy backgrounds.

Chapter 3: Cultural Foundations. Aspects of culture in ESL classrooms are discussed through perspectives on the concept of culture and cultural influences in second language classrooms and the culture of the school. Strategies for effective interaction and learning, for improving intercultural communication and working with the school and the community are discussed.

Chapter 4: English Language Proficiency. English language proficiency is defined as a multifaceted modality consisting of various levels of abilities and domains. Differences and similarities between language dominance and language proficiency are listed. Assessment is discussed holistically. A synopsis of currently available English language proficiency tests is listed.

Chapter 5: ESL Across Grade Levels. This chapter presents an overview of ESL programs on all levels of the curriculum including preschool, elementary, secondary levels as well as ESL for adults.

Chapter 6: ESL Programs. An examination of different ESL programs are listed. These are: free standing ESL in bilingual programs, survival, the work place, for specific purposes, and at the college level.

Chapter 7: Teaching Approaches. The chapter introduces the reader to several approaches of second language instruction that have been highly recommended by authorities in the field. Included in the chapter are: whole language, natural approach, total physical response, language experience approach. The emphasis is on combining, rather than selecting one of these approaches.

Chapter 8: Listening and Speaking. Listening and speaking play central roles in second language acquisition and development. Theory of listening comprehension and speaking as well as successful teaching strategies are described throughout the chapter.

Chapter 9: English Literacy. Literacy is described as the inclusion of decoding, interpreting and articulating messages within appropriate sociocultural contexts. A definition of literacy in ESL and the connection between language, reading, and writing are discussed. Specific attention is given to the many aspects to consider in teaching reading and writing to second language learners.

Chapter 10: Special Education. A significant number of limited English proficient students are enrolled in special education classrooms. Areas included are: assessment issues, the ESL learning disabled, the ESL mentally retarded, the ESL emotionally disabled and the ESL language disordered. Although the author is not quite comfortable with these labels, they were used for specificity purposes.

Chapter 11: The Human Factor. Parents, teachers and principals are influential human components in the ESL classroom. The chapter provides a brief overview of those human skills of teaching, administering, and parenting.

Chapter 12: ESL Resources. This chapter has two parts. The first part includes a selected list of organizations that have been nationally recognized for their effort in promoting theory, research and instruction in second language classrooms. The second part lists a directory of organizations who provide helpful resources to ESL educators.

This book evolved with the help of many persons. I would like to express my gratitude to all those individuals who contributed to the completion of this book, especially all those ESL teachers and Fordham University graduate TESOL and Bilingual Teacher Education students who inspired me in writing each of the chapters. Special recognition is given to those graduate students who allowed me to pilot the book and gave me many insights during the revising and editing stages. Lourdes and Ben Willems have my deep gratitude for patiently typing and retyping the manuscript. I thank my colleagues at Fordham University Graduate School of Education who encouraged me to finish this book. My special thanks go to Ruth Abrams, a doctoral student and a dedicated ESL teacher who was responsible for the final editing of the book. Finally, my husband Ceferino and my daughter Angeles Ivette deserve special recognition for their understanding and patience throughout its completion. At Garland, thanks to Mary Ellen Larcada who encouraged me to write this book and gave me the necessary enthusiasm to complete the work. To all of them, thank you.

Angela Carrasquillo

Teaching English as a Second Language

Chapter 1

Linguistic Foundations for Teaching English as a Second Language

Knowledge of English is a necessity in America and in the world. United States citizens and residents must understand, speak, read, and write English in order to survive and function in American society, in which English is the national tongue. English is essential for full participation in the academic, economic, and political system of the United States and perhaps in the world. English is the official spoken language of many other countries (Australia, Belize, Jamaica, South Africa, to mention some). English is an international language used for commercial, educational and general communication purposes. All individuals will benefit from becoming literate and proficient in English. This is the main reason that United States naturalization laws require candidates for citizenship to be able to speak English and demonstrate some degree of English literacy so that they might fully achieve membership in American society.

Schools in the United States have the moral and educational responsibility to promote and facilitate the learning of English. English as a second language (ESL) is one of the vehicles schools use to facilitate the acquisition of English. This chapter briefly discusses the linguistic foundations for teaching English to individuals whose native language is not English, or who come from environments where a language other than English is used for oral and written communication. The chapter provides a definition of the field of ESL, an overview of the nature of the language acquisition process as well as the trends in second language acquisition theory. This overview provides the linguistic background necessary to understand the following chapters.

ESL: A Definition

English as a second language (ESL), also referred to as English for speakers of other languages, is a specialized approach to language instruction designed for those who have a primary language other than English and who are limited in English proficiency. The term "specialized" connotes the use of several distinct and varying methods and strategies based on a wide range of innovative learning theories that have been developed over several decades, and which deal specifically with learning and teaching strategies of English to non-native or limited English speakers.

The application of the theories of linguistic science to the teaching of English as a second language has been increasing steadily since the 1940s.   This approach to language learning as a tool of verbal communication gained impetus during World War II when the United States government needed personnel with practical knowledge of foreign languages. It became necessary for the government to set up its own language training programs for military and civilian personnel who would be working in various parts of the world with people who spoke languages other than English. The wide spread use of tape recorders and other audio devices made it possible to provide authentic examples of spoken language.

By the early 1950s, teachers responsible for teaching English to non-English speakers were using some of the methodologies used in the military setting such as pattern practice techniques, use of meaning in oral practice, and the learning of language structures. In its early development, ESL teaching involved small numbers of foreign students in the United States who were taught only by specialized language teachers. But, in 1964 the federal government through Title IX of the National Defense Education Act (NDEA) officially recognized that, in addition to foreign students abroad, there were thousands of students in the United States whose native tongue was other than English and who needed specialized instruction in English if they were fully to understand or participate in the American cultural, social, and economic way of life. ESL programs grew through the NDEA. ESL programs included instruction in English at all levels including content in the students' culture. The aim of the instructional program was to assist non-English-speaking students designated as "disadvantaged" because they spoke a non-standard variety of English. Most of the ESL programs were offered at the adult/college level. Training in ESL methodology was provided for the preparation of ESL adult or college teachers.

English as a second language spread very rapidly, requiring teachers and professors to meet to discuss issues pertaining to the profession. The first of three ad-hoc conferences in TESOL was held in March of 1964. The professional organization TESOL (Teachers of English to Speakers of Other Languages) was established in 1966, the development of ESL textbooks increased, and several ESL methodologies were created. The organization was created out of professional concern over the lack of a single/all-inclusive professional organization that might bring together teachers and administrators at all educational levels with an interest in English for speakers of other languages. During these two decades, the ESL profession expanded in response to increasing members of immigrants and refugee children and youth entering the United States, as well as the growing number of foreign students coming from countries around the world to attend universities in the United States (Alatis, 1987).

A qualified ESL program is sensitive to second language learners' needs, experiences, native languages, and cultural backgrounds. Appropriate ESL instruction: (a) emphasizes communication and meaning; (b) integrates the four areas for functional contexts of learning and communication development: understanding, speaking, reading and writing; (c) recognizes students' prior linguistic, conceptual, and cultural experiences to build proficiency in English; (d) respects the values and traditions of students' cultural heritage, and (e) provides for continuation of conceptual development for functional contexts of learning and communication. The program provides adequate opportunity for the child to make adjustments to a new linguistic environment. It allows ESL learners to maintain self-esteem, and continue to develop academic areas; that is, before entering the mainstream curriculum, limited English proficient (LEP) students need to use English as a tool for learning subject matter.

The major objective of ESL programs is to prepare students to function successfully in classrooms where English is the medium of instruction for all subject areas. ESL instruction provides opportunities for students to learn English systematically and cumulatively moving from concrete to abstract levels of language. ESL includes instruction in all English communication skills; emphasizing the four basic aspects of the English language in order to communicate in an English environment. ESL students need to develop the ability to understand native speakers of English in any situation as well as the ability to read and write materials in English with comprehension and enjoyment. Thus, the general objective of an ESL program is the systematic development of the following areas:

- A vocabulary for expressing oneself in different social and academic environments.
- Automatic control and fluency in the use of natural and accurate English language, linguistic and grammatical patterns.
- Natural communication situations for meaningful interaction.
- Creative grammatical and syntactical construction abilities.
- Development of strategies to confront the process and varied skills of reading.
- Development of conceptual, grammatical, and syntactical forms of writing.

ESL is not a remedial program but a program designed to enhance and develop individuals' linguistic skills, cognitive skills and content area knowledge. The stigma of seeing ESL as remedial may have been caused by ESL "pull out" programs in which students receive from one hour to a half hour of instruction in segregated ESL centers or classes. An effective alternative is the "integrated approach," which relates language learning to content areas and directly provides comprehensible input to the LEP student and can bridge the gap that otherwise can divide language and the content classroom. An integrated approach helps to assure that LEP students use English as a tool for learning subject matter and helps them to progress to full academic proficiency (Short, 1991).

ESL teaching has been influenced mostly by two major approaches to the study of language: the behaviorist model and the cognitive model. These two models are briefly described below.

The Behaviorist Model

The behaviorist theory approach is based on the learning theory of the psychologist B. F. Skinner (1957) who cites the relevance of the stimulus response associations and mediating process in language learning. Skinner regarded human and animal behavior as determined largely by environmental circumstances. To demonstrate his point and to discover more about the influences of the environment on the learning process, Skinner and his followers, through their system called "behaviorism," taught different types of animals and people to acquire all sorts of behaviors—ranging from pigeons which became bombardiers, pill inspectors, and table-tennis players, to human beings who learned languages, mathematics, occupational tasks, social skills, and other behaviors to a significant level of achievement through these methods. Skinner's basic principle was immediate positive reinforcement. Skinner's theory, presented in the academic scene in the 1940s and early 1950s, presented the notion that language acquisition, first and second, is a phenomenon attributable to habit formation, to rote, to stimulus, to response, to conditions. Language is a learned behavior, a system of habits by means of which verbal behavior is developed through a continuation of stimulus-responses and reinforcement of patterns.

Language was viewed as a collection of discrete items to be put together like building blocks. Language was to be learned through mimicry, memorization, and analogy. Language methodologies concentrated heavily on structures and patterns of the "forms" of language. As a result, the techniques used by teachers were often in part mechanical. The techniques emphasized listening and speaking; but reading and writing were to be introduced later in the language development process.

The behaviorist approach took ESL teaching into the audiolingual approach. Proponents of this model emphasized that initial language study takes the form of memorization of dialogues, which are composed of useful situational utterances that can be varied to meet a number of conversational needs within the target culture. Students learn to give responses to the stimuli of the dialogue sentences, at first in the exact form memorized, then with variations. Grammar was learned through drilling in substitution, expansion, and conversion of elements in the language patterns. Reading was introduced systematically, beginning with the reading of what has been learned orally, with careful attention to sound-symbol correspondence. Writing was seen as a supportive exercise to oral learning in the early stages.   The behaviorist orientation of language acquisition was challenged in the 1960s.   The main challenges came from the linguistic theories current at that time and from cognitive psychologists.

The Cognitive Model

In the early 1960s, criticisms were heard against the behavioristic theory of language learning.   Criticisms were made of the overemphasis of tedious, mechanistic processes leaving little room for language learners' spontaneous understanding of the crucial elements of language. Chomsky (1965), in the introductory chapter of *Aspects of the Theory of Syntax,* indicated that he was challenging behavioristic theories of language acquisition. According to Chomsky, language learning is not a matter of habit and conditioning, but a creative process—a rationalistic and cognitive activity.   It was proposed that human beings have an innate propensity for language acquisition.   Thus, language is the product of genetics and evolution, and the human organism has an inherent capacity to process linguistic data (Chomsky, 1965). This model emphasizes the creative aspect of language use, the universality of underlying linguistic structures, along with the notion that children work out rules from the input available to them.   Perception, memory, thinking, how meaning is encoded and expressed, and how information is processed became areas of major concern.

Chomsky (1957; 1965) hypothesized that children acquire a language by making hypotheses about the form of the grammar of the language with which they are surrounded. Children can compare this with their innate knowledge of possible grammar based on the principles of universal grammar. For Chomsky, language is this wide-governed behavior that enables speakers to create new utterances that conform to the rules they have internalized. And, as Rivers (1988) says: "The terms 'rule-governed behavior,' 'creative language use,' and 'hypothesis testing,' soon replaced 'building in habits' and 'saturation practice' as the catchwords of language teaching" (pp. 6-7).

In response, at least in part to Chomsky's cognitive model, major language learning methods ensued or developed which contrast vividly with the "Audiolingual Method," such as "The Natural Learning Approach" and "Communicative Language Teaching." In "Communicative Language Teaching," for example, meaning—not form—is paramount and dialogues center around communicative roles; dialogues are not memorized, and if drilling is done at all, it is done peripherally. Any tool which helps the learner may be used. Whereas the "Audiolingual Method" stresses linguistic competence, "Communicative Language Teaching" stresses communicative competence (Richards & Rodgers, 1986). In recent years, the cognitive model has tended to replace the behaviorist model in second language teaching.

The Nature of Language Acquisition

Language is an arbitrary system of symbols by which thought is conveyed from one human being to another. This definition emphasizes a number of important aspects of language:

1. *Language is the most impressive expression of human beings.* Every physiologically and mentally normal person acquires in childhood the ability to make use of a system of vocal communication, as both speaker and hearer. According to language experts, speakers possess abstract abilities that enable them to produce grammatically correct sentences in a language. Children actively engage in a gradual subconscious and creative process of discovery through which they acquire the rule systems of their language.

2. *Language is used to interact or communicate with other members of the same speech community.* The process of first-language acquisition as a spoken medium of communication is largely achieved through exposure to the language. Meaning is the key to linguistic development, and creativity is very important in the process of language acquisition. This creative aspect of language comprehension and production makes it hard to realize its extent, but it is simply part of what is expected in the maturation process. Individuals do not have any difficulty in understanding almost everything they hear everyday and producing sentences to suit the requirements of everyday situations. Puerto Rican

Spanish speakers can interact or communicate without difficulty with Spanish speakers from Spain, Argentina, or any other Spanish-speaking country. English speakers of the United States can communicate with English speakers from Jamaica, England, or Australia. Normally, people acquire as their first language the language spoken by their parents or by those with whom they are brought up from infancy. An exception to this principle is when parents use different languages at home, and children grow up in a bilingual home setting and are able to communicate in more than one language.

3. *Language is a means of individual expression.* Individuals use language to impart information, express feelings and emotions, and to influence the activities of others. The language produced has a particular purpose, for example, to convey a need, to accomplish a task such as getting an object, to express feelings such as joy or sadness. Language is also used to share friendliness or hostility towards persons who make use of a similar set of voices.

4. *To some extent, language is transmitted culturally; that is, it is a social phenomenon.* Language conveys the idea of the relation of words and concepts between individuals of the same cultural group. Children learn languages by listening to others and imitating those vocal symbols that make sense to them in their own cultural, mental, and creative process. Language is culturally transmitted in the home and family environment, and the best way in which adults can help young language learners is by giving them guidance and encouragement (Wells, 1986). Wells (1986) states that: "children progressively construct a representation of the language of their community. And they do this on the basis of the evidence provided for them in conversation with more mature members of that community" (p. 44). However, language is an abstract entity that cannot be completely molded by external forces. Language is derived from the knowledge that is already resident in the individual surrounded by a rich and stimulating language environment.

5. *Language normally does not operate without meaning or function.* Children are meaning makers, always trying to make sense of their world (Wells, 1986). For example, Wells says that children are "seekers after meaning who try to find the

underlying principles that will account for the patterns that they recognize in their experiences" (p. 43). Because children are active, constructive learners, they are constantly solving problems and generating and testing hypotheses. The development of comprehension starts when children begin to understand the meaning of the language they are using, especially through experimentation. Language learners are learning all the time, using social and cognitive strategies. Initially, word or phrase meaning is vague to children. With experience, however, children come to know the names of things and the characteristics of various concepts. Long after children use a word or a phrase, they are still acquiring attributes and experiencing the meaning of that word or phrase. The acquisition of meanings and concepts is a process that continues well beyond the early years.

6. *Language production is usually less than language comprehension.* Language learners show more receptive language than the language they are able to produce. Perceptually, children need to have some comprehension of the language system that they are trying to internalize. Psychologically, children must feel comfortable about using the language productively. Once they feel ready to express their thoughts orally, they will communicate in the language.

Stages in language acquisition have been identified. These include *pre-production*, in which beginners develop ability to understand meaning; *early production*, in which the ability to speak develops, usually with single words and stock phrases; *speech emergence*, in which more elaborate speech is generated; and *intermediate fluency*, in which students begin to engage in conversation, producing full sentences and connecting them in a narrative context.

Language Acquisition in Children

Language acquisition is a developmental changing process lasting throughout a lifetime, starting at birth or earlier and continuing into the classroom setting where the child's creative process is encouraged and expanded. Children have a deep, genetically-transmitted tendency toward speech. Linguistic research continues to investigate the process of how children acquire language. It is amazing to see how children acquire such a complex system of symbols at an early stage of development. It is a monumental task to acquire and express grammatical structures that are saturated by underlying semantic relations and grammatical categories. Given linguistic stimulation, most children acquire language. Regardless of race, class or family background, children learn their native language during infancy and the preschool years with ease and success. Without formal instruction, children learn the structure of the language and use it for numerous communicative purposes. They learn language within a natural environment of language use. Students' ability to organize the new language system depends largely on how well they can understand what they hear. When students are at the early stages of learning how to speak a new language, they know few words in the language and therefore need to see the meaning of what they hear. Concrete referents for verbal input are important ingredients of a learner's early language environment.

Children learn language not simply by imitating adults but also by testing construction and creative utterances (Chomsky, 1957, 1965; Wells, 1986). These behaviors are transformed or modified when language has a personal meaning for children, such as communicating a special activity or purpose. Children talk mostly for functional purposes: to ask; to get information; to inform; to express anger or surprise; or to express a need, such as hunger or cold. If there is not a functional need to use the language, the children will not express interest in and be motivated to use the language.

Authorities such as Brown (1987), Chomsky (1957, 1965), Goodman & Goodman (1981), and Smith (1971) suspect that language is universally acquired in the same manner. Infants gradually master the rules that help them to produce grammatical utterances of the language spoken around them. A child learns to talk by being immersed in spoken language. Children learn the language by relating their understanding of the new to what they already know and by changing the knowledge they acquire. Children remember and use language that is meaningful. They learn through a creative construction process of putting together the language they know. Children use a great amount of language and make at least some sense of it before they are ready to attempt to speak it. Learners begin to express their meaning through an interlanguage which is an approximation of the adult or native speaker model and which contains many omissions, generalizations, and errors in grammar, pronunciation, and vocabulary. At the beginning, it reflects telegraphic speech (a stage in language development in which all but the essential words of an utterance are omitted) in many ways. An example of telegraphic speech is "Mommy give cookie" for "Mommy give me one of those cookies."

Language development is an essential part of children's growth. Experimentation with language is a source of pride and delight as children acquire the complexities of linguistic structures and progress from simpler to more complex grammatical forms. In the process, they acquire the competence to communicate effectively in different social contexts. Children need to listen to a great deal of language in order for the language to make sense before they are ready to attempt to speak it. The most effective language learning environment provides natural communication with peers on meaningful topics and experiences. The stages through which children move in this interlanguage are the same for many children, although there are individual differences in the order of acquisition of certain structures. At the beginning, language learners produce a great deal of incomplete or incorrect language, which they gradually correct themselves as they try to match their language to the models they hear.

Language Development in Adolescence and Beyond

Language development research has traditionally focused on early childhood, leaving practitioners to question if there is any further language development during the adolescent or later years. But oral and written language continue to develop interwovenly as the child advances into adulthood. As with oral skills, written language flourishes and improves when adolescents are part of communities that use print to transfer meaningful messages. During adolescence, young people acquire their own special style; "part of being a successful teenager lies in knowing how to talk like one" (Gleason, 1989; p. 5). The teens' formation of identity, their own sense of self is a major focus for adolescents' language during this period of their lives.

Since social meaning is so important, adolescents and adults tend to use language that solidifies them with their register or peer group (Obler, 1988). Adolescents use specific styles of language to insure their separation from both the social group of children and adults.

Obler (1988) calls this phenomenon "bonding language." Danesi (1989) studied 36 adolescents (ages 13 to 18) via the use of tape recordings and interviews. Three distinct styles of language were employed by adolescents: "emotive language programming," "connotative language programming," and "socially coded language programming." "Emotive language programming" emphasizes the strong feelings expressed by adolescents and is characterized through increased rates of speech, overwrought intonation, simplified clause structure and expressive voice modulation enhanced by gestures and facial expressions. This style is used both with peers and adults. In "connotative language programming" adolescents coin words or phrases or extend meanings of existing ones (loser, gross, air head, slime bucket). This style of speech is used primarily with peers. "Socially coded language programming" is characterized by abundant use of swear words. The swear words do not hold the same vulgar connotations of adult usage, but become socially coded speech features of the adolescent's language, suggesting that adolescents are not only conscious of how they are perceived in their dress but also how they are perceived linguistically.

Another aspect of adolescents' language is gender related. Adolescents are very much aware of the linguistic structures appropriate to their gender. Since identity is so important for this age group, it is very common to see them acting within the norms of the sex-specific peer group. For example males often use non-standard forms of speech such as "she do," and they are much more prone to interrupt females than the reverse. In like manner, girls' conversations are much more intimate and their speech style generates equality through the use of the word form "we" (Obler, 1988; Cooper & Anderson-Inman, 1988).

Peer groups are also bound by a common language (Cooper & Anderson-Inman, 1988; Danesi, 1989). Obler (1988) extends Danesi's research to peer groups of all ages. She states that adults need to acquire styles of speech in their work and social relationships. People of similar occupations often seek each other out because the language (jargon) used in their field of work establishes a peer group. Likewise, one uses a different language in different social settings, i.e. wine tasting, football game. Demonstrating this control over linguistic features and competence in language enhances the likelihood of being accepted by a certain peer group. Cooper & Anderson-Inman (1988) cited a study by Hewitt (1987) in which white adolescents used Creole in an attempt to establish in-group relations between speakers of different ethnic backgrounds. White adolescents using Creole were accepted by the black kids who used it as a source of their identity. Thus, social oral language and oral figurative language support the adolescent's need to play with language and use language to feel like part of a social group.

Research on reading and writing development in a child's adolescent years is scarce. The few studies conducted on this age level reveal that reading and writing in adolescence also develop linguistically and socially. Reading is most significant to the adolescents' language growth, as it extends the various levels of literacy in which adolescents develop sources of knowledge, cognitive and metacognitive strategies for processing and producing diverse texts, utilizing both literal and figurative meaning (Nelson, 1988). Major characteristics of early adolescent readers are presented in Early's (1984) work. She concluded that early adolescents' oral reading is typically accurate and fluent and literal reading comprehension skills have been mastered. Middle schoolers also tend to be confused by metaphors and symbols in literature. For most, figurative/abstract thinking is achieved in later adolescence. And most important, many adolescents do not spend time reading.

Adolescents' writing encompasses meaning and structure as well as preoccupation for audience function and purpose. Syntactic complexity is reflected in adolescents' writing since sentence length, types of conjunctions, and number of phrases and clauses increase as adolescents gain more facility with language (Scott, 1988). Noun and verb phrases become more complex, and adverbial connectives such as "therefore" are used more readily as they get older.

In sum, learning involves meaning and for many adolescents meaning is achieved through verbal participation, functional reading and creative writing. ESL programs developed for adolescents should recognize the need to understand the unique characteristics of adolescents' language and incorporate instructional strategies that meet these language characteristics.

The Second Language Acquisition Process

The term "second language" became popular in the 1960s as the result of the new awareness of the language diversity that exists in the United States and in the world. The acquisition of a second language is an activity undertaken mostly when children, youths, or adults have already nearly or fully acquired the basic structure and vocabulary of their first language. Acquisition of a second language is a gradual process involving the mapping of meaning and use. Second language acquisition requires meaning by interaction in which speakers are concerned not with the form of their utterances but with the understanding of the messages they are conveying (Krashen, 1981). Meaning is the key to second language linguistic development; children remember and use the language that is meaningful. Children use language to understand and to communicate meaning. They learn through a creative process of putting together the pieces of the language they know.

The literature on the acquisition of a second language makes a distinction as to whether the two languages are acquired from the simultaneous experience of the use of both in the same circumstances and settings, or by exposure to each language used in different settings and at different times. Research on second language acquisition has tried to answer many questions about the nature of the process. Among these questions, those which are dealt with most in the literature are: (a) Does the process of second language acquisition follow the same stages as the first? (b) Do children learn the second language the same as adults do? (c) Does age play a key role in second language acquisition? (d) Are first language skills transferable to the second language? and (e) How do individual differences affect the acquisition of the second language? During the last thirty years, theories about the nature of second language learning and learning processes have been changing in some very fundamental ways, presenting different views or adding additional components to the above questions. The following paragraphs present a synopsis of current views of the second language acquisition process. This is not to say that every language researcher or theorist agrees with these current views but that a significant group of them tend to agree on the nature and the process of the acquisition of a second language.

On the issue of similarities between first and second language learning, it appears that children acquiring a target language follow the same developmental sequence of linguistic patterns as children acquiring a native one, although differences do exist as in first language acquisition. Children tend to acquire simpler forms first and progress to the more complex grammatical forms, even when they differ in age at the time of second language acquisition. Second language learners learn through a creative construction process of putting together the bits of the language they know rather than by exact imitation of sentence models. Children begin to express their meaning through an interlanguage which is an approximation of the adult or native-speaker model, and which may contain many omissions, overgeneralizations, and errors in grammar, pronunciation and vocabulary (Chamot & Stewner, 1985). In many ways, it appears like telegraphic speech, since words which are not essential to the meaning are routinely omitted. The stages through which children move in this interlanguage are almost the same for all children who are learning a language. Children do not begin by communicating complete, grammatically-correct sentences. At the beginning, they produce a lot of incorrect language which they gradually correct as they try to match their language to the language models they hear.

Research evidences some differences between first and second language acquisition. Second language learners are more cognitively developed and have already experienced learning a language, demonstrating a great amount of linguistic knowledge. Second language learners build on their cognitive and linguistic knowledge to learn the second language more effectively. A quick answer to the question of differences between adult and child second language learners is that the language process is similar and different. Hakuta (1986) argues that child and adult second language acquisition is qualitatively similar, but factors such as language attitude and intelligence account for differences.

The issue of age which is directly tied to the above question is a controversial one in second language acquisition theory. Theories pertaining to the optimal age to begin learning a second language suggest that something in the early development of the child maximizes the probability that the younger the human organism when exposed to a language, the greater the probability that the individual will acquire a native pronunciation (Lenneberg, 1967). But research indicates that there is no direct evidence that a child has a special language learning capacity which is absent in the adult (Asher & Garcia, 1982).

Transferability of skills from one language to another appears to play a critical role in second language acquisition. Transfer of knowledge and language skills from one language to another could contribute to the acquisition of a second language. However, there is almost no research evidence on which to determine which specific skills are easily transferable from one language to the other and their effects on learning the second language. There are differences between the process of first and second language acquisition. Two of the most frequently mentioned in the literature are age and individual differences. One of the big differences between learning a first and second language is the factor of age, i.e. the chronological age in which each language is introduced and the amount of time the learner is exposed to the second language. There are differences between a child of one or two years of age learning the native language and a child of ten years learning the second language. Cognitive and social factors are quite different in both children. For example, much of a younger child's language acquisition takes place in infancy and in the pre-school years. The older learner is cognitively more mature and has different social needs than the younger child.

Learners acquire a second language through stages. Through these stages, second language learners:

1. Establish social relationships with the speakers of the target language. Children engage in interacting activities, and in informational activities. Children rely on listening comprehension and non-verbal communication. Behaviors of this stage include: (a) communicating with gestures and actions, (b) focusing on listening comprehension, and (c) building receptive vocabulary.

2. Concentrate on speaking the second language. This is a creative stage in which children combine semantic, syntactic and grammatical formulas to communicate in the target language. Behaviors of this stage include: (a) speaking using one or two words or short phrases, (b)

expanding receptive vocabulary, (c) producing vocabulary they understand, and (d) using language to communicate needs or interests.

3. Progress in communicating in all forms in the target language. Behaviors of this stage include: (a) speaking in longer phrases or sentences, (b) continuing to expand receptive vocabulary, (c) producing high levels of language use, (d) using various forms of language (oral, reading, writing), (e) producing connected narratives, (f) continuing to expand vocabulary, and (g) using various forms of language for expressing and learning.

These stages are reflected in the cognitive and social strategies children use. For example, they seek out peers who speak the language being learned. They enjoy role-playing and games, and they are uninhibited when speaking their second language. It is important for second-language learners to be allowed to communicate even if they make mistakes while doing so.

Describing second language acquisition is a complex task since there are many variables that need to be addressed. To summarize the nature and process of second language acquisition, the following language principles are listed along with examples of use, often inappropriately considered "wrong" rather than as manifestations of language in the process of development. These language principles have been mentioned in the literature as important variables in the second language acquisition process:

1. *First and second language learners apply very similar strategies in the language acquisition process.* Some of these strategies are:
   a. The use of simple structures when constructing sentences. One commonly used structure is following a construction order of subject plus verb plus object. An example is **Me feed cat** for **I feed the cat. I a student** for **I am a student.**
   b. The use of simple structures before more complex ones. An example is **Me no go** for **I don't want to go.**
   c. The use of overextending the meanings of words. An example is using the words **long** and **short** as similar to **big** and **small.**

    d. Disregarding past tenses. An example is **I go to the movies yesterday** for **I went to the movies yesterday.**

    e. Overgeneralization of rules. An example is when the children say **You doed** for **You did.** The overgeneralization is that all the past tense of verbs end with *ed.*

2. *Errors are a natural part of language learning.* Language acquisition is not based on grammatical structures but on meaning. When speakers have something interesting or meaningful to communicate, the listener will make every effort to understand. This very effort will advance the second language acquisition process. Language learners do not have to have a conscious awareness of the "rules" they do or do not possess. Acquirers may self-correct only on the basis of a "feel" for grammatically correct forms (Krashen, 1981). With the exception of pronunciation, most second language errors are similar to first language errors.

3. *Language learners go through a silent period before they begin to orally produce the language.* Since children acquire language in meaningful situations, speech emerges in natural stages. Children usually show a "pre-production period" in which they can begin to comprehend but say very little (Terrell, 1981). This silent stage helps children to concentrate on the message that is being conveyed to them. In this initial stage, children may concentrate on listening for comprehension, or perhaps in reading comprehension.

4. *Motivation influences the speed and ease of acquiring a second language.* Positive attitudes toward the target language encourage useful and comprehensible input for language acquisition (Krashen, 1981). It allows the acquirer to be open to input which can be utilized for acquisition. For example, the desire to be like valued members of the community that speak the second language and the desire to achieve proficiency in the target language for utilitarian or practical reasons, are aspects that have been positively related to second-language acquisition.

5. *Language learning represents a collaborative meaning making process* (Wells, 1986). Successful second language learners effectively use interpretation, expression, and negotiation of meaning. Language is learned interactively and in context.

Listening, reading, speaking, and writing are all active language components, interrelated skills in the process of oral and written communication.

6. *There are individual variations among second language learners.* Social and psychological factors have an important bearing on the second language learning process. Variables such as motivation, attitude, aptitude, and cognitive/learning style influence second language learners' growth in the target language.

7. *Second learners' goals and empowerment skills are essential in the process of second language acquisition.* Successful learners share a sense of confidence-building, ego-enhancing, a quest for competence in some domain of knowledge or skill (Brown, 1991). Learners need to be empowered to do language for their own personal reasons of achieving competence and autonomy (Brown, 1991). Brown (1991) states that English language classes in the 1990s are showing signs of providing such empowerment by shifting towards "(a) a focus on process, (b) egalitarian structures, (c) flexible, open-ended curricula, (d) gauging competence and potential, (e) encouraging calculated guessing, and (f) valuing synthesis and intuition" (p. 249).

8. *Language helps to perpetuate culture, and as a tool for that purpose is vitally connected to a person's cognitive and affective development.* Thus it is deemed beneficial, in acquiring the second language, to validate and preserve the first culture, so that optimal transference can take place.

The above second language principles help language educators to: (a) expect errors and consider them as indicators of children's language development; (b) provide context and action oriented activities to clarify meanings and functions of the new language; (c) provide opportunities for listening activities and wait for children to speak when they are ready; (d) plan activities to lessen anxiety among second language learners; (e) introduce language that is meaningful, natural, useful, and relevant to children; and, (f) recognize the importance of validating first language culture and language skills.

An Overview of Trends in Second Language Theory

Research in second language learning and teaching has been influenced by research on first language. In the last fifty years, language educators have been involved in describing the language learning process, and its stages and implementation in the classroom. There are different views depending on the language view of the time in which the research or theory was developed (Richards & Rodgers, 1986). The following is a brief overview of the trends in research and second language acquisition. This overview does not evaluate the merits of each theory, it only describes theoretical foundations and teaching principles.

Contrastive Analysis Theory

During the 1940s and the early 1950s, language teaching emphasis was on the comparison and contrast between the structure of the native language and the structure of the language being learned. This was called the "contrastive analysis approach." Phonological and grammatical patterns between the native and the second language were pointed out to the learners to help them to establish relationships between both languages. Brown (1987) indicated that "the contrastive analysis hypothesis" stressed the interfering effects of the first language in second-language learning and claimed, in its strong form, that second language learning is primarily, if not exclusively, a process of acquiring whatever items are different from the first language" (p. 168). Lado (1957) in the preface to the book *Linguistics Across Cultures* said: "The plan of the book rests on the assumption that we can predict and describe the patterns that will cause difficulty in learning, and those that will not cause difficulty, by comparing systematically the language and culture to be learned with the native language and culture of the student" (p. vii).

Contrastive analysis research contrasted the system of one language, the grammar, the phonology and the lexicon with the system of the second language in order to predict those difficulties which speakers of the second language would have in learning the target language and to construct teaching materials to help them learn that language. The selection of the items presented to learn a language was dependent upon the outcomes of a contrastive analysis–a systematic comparison between the native language and the second language so that areas which could prove troublesome would be identified in advance and be given special attention.

Error Analysis Theory

Error analysis was a response to the controversy developed by the contrastive approach in the 1950s and the 1960s. It is defined as the identification of the differences between the way people learning a language speak and the way native speakers of the language use the language (Richards, 1971, 1974). By looking at children's speech, comparing it with adult speech, and trying to account for the differences, language researchers speculated about the nature of the mental processes that seem to be involved in language. The high frequency occurrence of these types of errors in the speech of young children were considered to be an example of the way grammar and linguistic proficiency emerge in the speech of second language learners. These errors were seen as evidence of second language learners being active participants in the acquisition of language (Hakuta and Cancino, 1977). Among the most general errors found were: overgeneralization, ignorance of rule restrictions, incomplete application of rules and false concepts hypothesized. In this context, Richards (1971) concluded that although interference from the first language is clearly a major source of difficulty in second language learning, many errors derive from the strategies employed by the learner in the process of language acquisition (development), and from the mutual interference of items within the target language.

Linguistic Performance Theory

At the same time that second language researchers were concentrating on error analysis, researchers of first language were developing new methodologies for the study of linguistic performance. Chomsky (1965) asserted that children come into the world with innate language-learning abilities. Consequently, children acquire language by making hypotheses about the form of the grammar of the language with which they are surrounded. They then compare this with their innate knowledge of possible grammar based on the principles of universal grammar. In this way, children internalize a knowledge of the grammar of the native language (this Chomsky called "competence") and this grammar makes language use (or performance) possible.   Studies of performance analysis have concentrated on three categories: acquisition of negation, acquisition of grammatical morphemes, and acquisition of "prefabricated utterances" (Cazden, 1972). Cazden emphasized that there are many factors to be considered in performance analysis. For example,

> "communicative competence" includes both knowledge of language (in the more usual and narrow sense of syntax, phonology, and semantics) and knowledge of the social world and of rules for using language in that world...these aspects of communicative competence are realized in the child's actual speech behavior, or performance. This performance includes both speaking and comprehending. (p. 3)

The study of the acquisition of negation by Klima and Bellugi (1966) provided the methodology to search for universal orders of acquisition of structure across second language learners and the role of language transfer.

Discourse Analysis Theory

The late 1970s and the beginning of the 1980s provided the "acquisition of discourse theory" (the flow and the structure of a conversation or topics within).   Language or conversation was analyzed and described in terms of meaning, form, and substance (discourse, syntax, and phonology).   The discourse analysis theory emphasizes that it is necessary to know what is acquired and used in order to indicate parameters and scope on the language acquisition patterns in second language learners.   Hatch (1978) posed the basic assumption of this theory by saying:

> It is assumed that one first learns how to manipulate structures, that one gradually builds up a repertoire of structures and then, somehow, learns how to put the structures to use in discourse. We would like to consider the possibility that just the reverse happens. One learns how to do conversation, one learns how to interact verbally, and out of this interaction syntactic structures are developed. (p. 404)

Interlanguage Analysis Theory

By the mid 1970s, second language researchers began to use the term "interlanguage" to describe the systematic language second language learners were using at a particular stage of learning, that is, the learners' version of second language which deviated in certain ways from the target forms. This interlanguage was seen as an indication that second language learners were testing hypotheses about the forms of grammar in the new language. Presumably, when interlanguage speakers produced utterances that were not comprehended by speakers of the language, they would eject their former hypotheses and develop others, gradually bringing their interlanguage into closer conformity to the accepted forms of the second language. Selinker (1974) identified meaningful performance situations relevant to interlanguage identifications in: (a) utterances in the learners' native language; (b) interlanguage utterances produced by second language speakers; and (c) utterances produced by native speakers of the target language. Rivers (1988) said that :

> Controversy raged as to whether deviant forms in the interlanguage were the result of interference, or negative transfer, from the L1 of the L2 learner or were developmental errors of the same type as those to be observed in the interim grammars of young children learning this language as a first language. (pp. 10-11)

Cognitive Language Theory

In the late 1970s, cognitive psychologists analyzed cognitive operations that language users performed. The trend toward a more active use of the language learners' mental powers probably represents the most important effect of the cognitive theory of language acquisition. Cognitive learning psychology holds that any act of learning involves the relating or integrating of all new information into the individuals' theory of the world, a theory constructed by the individuals themselves on the basis of all past experiences. This language learning approach tries to describe what goes on inside the thought processing apparatuses: how children observe, interpret, relate, interrelate, comprehend and produce language, and how they reorganize and use materials for learning (Piaget & Inhelder, 1958,

1968).   According to Piaget all cognitive acquisition, including language is the outcome of a gradual process of construction. Children gradually are more able to make sense of the world and are constantly constructing new levels of cognitive organization as they mature.   Viewing language learning as a natural creative process suggests that second language learners should be provided opportunities to think in the language, rather than merely use repetitive drills.

One of the most accepted language theories in this movement was the concept of language learning through content.   Learners use content as they use language.   Instead of teaching language isolated from the subject matter, language development is integrated with content learning.   Language is seen not only as a means of communication but as a medium of learning.

Natural Language Learning Theory

The "natural language learning approach" (also called the Developmental Approach) has its roots in an older approach developed in the middle of the nineteenth century to simulate in the classroom an environment that will approximate the context in which children acquire their first language. This latest form, popularized by Krashen (1981) and Terrell (1981), has emphasized communicative interaction as the most important activity in the acquisition of a language. The basic principle of "natural language learning" is the distinction Krashen and Terrell have established between "acquisition" of a language and "learning" of a language. Language acquisition is a subconscious process; language acquirers are not usually aware that they are acquiring language but are only aware of the fact that they are using the language for communication. On the other hand, learning is a conscious learning of the second language, knowing the rules, being aware of them, and being able to talk about them.

In the natural approach, much listening to the language is advocated   before   production   is   expected   and   encouraged. Recommended techniques are physical responses to instruction and simple verbal and non-verbal responses to pictures or comments by the teacher or other language users. The proponents of natural language learning maintain that, through these techniques, the innate capacities to acquire a language that all individuals have will be tapped. Students will have ample opportunities to test their hypotheses about the new language. Their interim grammar will be accepted while they are refining their hypotheses through experience in communication. Through a process of "creative construction" and "comprehensible input" second language learners will acquire and expand the second language.

Communicative Language Theory

Sociolinguistics, a language movement of the 1960s and 1970s, concentrates on language as it is used for communication within the social group. Hymes (1972) reacted to Chomsky's characterization of the linguistic competence of the ideal native speaker and proposed the term "communicative competence" to represent the use of language in social context, and the observance of sociolinguistic norms of appropriacy. Savignon (1972, 1983) used the term to characterize the ability of language learners to interact with other speakers to make meaning of the language being used.

The focus of communicative competence has been the elaboration and implementation of programs and methodologies that promote the development of functional languages through learners' participation in communicative events in which second language learners communicate with speakers of the target language. Rivers (1988) expanding on the role of communicative language said:

> ...they need also to know the culturally acceptable ways of interacting orally with others–appropriate levels of language for different situations and different relationships; conversational openers and gambits and when it was appropriate to use these, how to negotiate meaning in various circumstances, and when and how to use appropriate gestures and body language; the message content of pitch, loudness, and intonation patterns, the questions and comments that were acceptable and unacceptable in the culture; and the importance of distance in communicative encounters. (p. 15)

The communicative approach to language provides for a variety of language activities which focus on communication and the expression and interpretation of meaning. Language educators have the flexibility to focus on meaningful and communicative tasks.

References

Alatis, J. E. (1987). The early history of TESOL. *TESOL Quarterly, 21*(2), 4-6.

Asher, J. J. & Garcia, R. (1982). The optimal age to learn a foreign language. In S. D. Krashen, R. C. Scarcella & M. H. Long (Eds.), *Child adult differences in second language acquisition* (pp. 3-19). Rowley, MA: Newbury House.

Brown, D. (1987). *Principles of language learning and teaching.* Englewood Cliffs, NJ: Prentice-Hall.

Brown, H. D. (1991). TESOL at twenty-five: What are the issues? *TESOL Quarterly, 25*(2), 245-260.

Cazden, C. B. (1972). *Child language and education.* New York: Holt & Rinehart.

Chamot, A. & Stewner, M. G. (1985). A summary of current literature on English as a second language. Report submitted to the U. S. Department of Education, Office of Bilingual Education and Minority Language Affairs. Contract No. 300840166. Rosslyn, VA: N.C.B.E.

Chomsky, N. (1957). *Syntactic structures.* The Hague: Mouton.

Chomsky, N. (1965). *Aspects of the theory of syntax.* Cambridge, MA: M.I.T. Press.

Cooper, D. & Anderson-Inman, L. (1988). Language and socialization. In M. Nippold (Ed.), *Late language development ages nine to nineteen* (pp. 225-246). Austin, TX: Pro-Ed.

Danesi, M. (1989). Adolescent language as affectively coded behavior. Findings of an observational research project. *Adolescence, 24*(94), 311-319.

Early, M. (1984). *Reading to learn in grades 5-12.* New York: Harcourt Brace Jovanovich.

Gleason, J. B. (1989). Studying language development. In J. B. Gleason (Ed.), *The development of language* (pp. 1-34). Columbus, OH: Merrill.

Goodman, K. & Goodman, Y. (Fall, 1981). *Twenty questions about language learning.* Educational Leadership, 2-7.

Hakuta, K. & Cancino, H. (1977). *Trends in second language acquisition research.* Harvard Educational Review, 47, 3, 294-316.

Hakuta, K. (1986). Mirror of language. New York: Basic Books.

Hatch, E. M. (1978). Discourse analysis and second language acquisition. In E. M. Hatch (Ed.), *Second language acquisition: A book of readings* (401-435). Rowley, MA: Newbury House.

Hymes, D. (1972). *On communicative competence.* In J. B. Pride & J. Holmes (Eds.), *Sociolinguistics* (pp. 269-293). Harmondsworth: Penguin.

Klima, E. & Bellugi, V. (1966). *Syntactic regularities in the speed of children.* In R. Wales (Ed.), Psycholinguistic papers (183-208). Edinburgh: Edinburgh University Press.

Krashen, S. (1981). *Second language acquisition.* Oxford, England: Pergamon Press Ltd.

Lado, R. (1957). *Linguistics across cultures.* Ann Arbor, MI: University of Michigan Press.

Lenneberg, E. H. (1967). Understanding language without ability to speak: A case report. *Journal of Abnormal and Social Psychology, 65,* 419-425.

Nelson, N. W. (1988). The nature of literacy. In M. A. Nippold (Ed.), *Late language development: Ages nine through nineteen* (97-127).

Austin, TX: Pro-Ed.

Piaget, J. & Inhelder, B. (1958). *The growth of logical thinking from childhood to adolescence.* New York: Basic Books.

Piaget, J. & Inhelder, B. (1969). *The psychology of the child.* London: Routledge.

Obler, L. (1988). Language beyond childhood. In J. B. Gleason (Ed.), *The development of language* (pp. 275-301). Columbus, OH: Merrill.

Richards, J. C (1971). A Non-contrastive Approach to Error Analysis. *English Language Teaching Journal, 25,* 204-219.

Richards, J. C (1974). Error analysis and second language strategies. In J. H. Schumann & N. Stenson (Eds.), *New frontiers in second language learning* (pp. 32-53). Rowley, MA: Newbury House.

Richards, J. C. & Rodgers, T. S. (1986). *Approaches and methods in language teaching: A description and analysis.* Cambridge, MA: Cambridge University Press.

Rivers, W. M. (1988). *Communicating naturally in a second language: Theory and practice in language teaching.* New York: Cambridge University Press.

Savignon, S. (1972). *Communicative competence: An experiment in foreign-language teaching.* Philadelphia: Center for Curriculum Development.

Savignon, S. (1983). *Communicative competence: Theory and classroom practice.* Reading, MA: Addison-Wesley.

Scott, C. M. (1988). Spoken and written syntax. In M. A. Nippold. *Late language development: Ages nine through nineteen* (pp. 49-96). Austin, TX: Pro-Ed.

Selinker, L. (1974). Interlanguage. In J. H. Schumann & N. Stenson

(Eds.), *New frontiers in second language learning* (pp. 114-136). Rowley, MA: Newbury House.

Short, D. (1991). *Integrating language and content instruction: Strategies and techniques.* Washington, DC: National Clearing House for Bilingual Education.

Skinner, B. F. (1957). *Verbal behavior.* New York: Appleton-Century Crofts.

Smith, F. (1971). *Understanding reading.* New York: Holt, Rinehart and Winston.

Terrell, T. D. (1981). The natural approach in bilingual education. In California State Department of Education (Ed.), *Schooling and language minority students: A theoretical framework* (pp. 117-146). Los Angeles, CA: Evaluation, Dissemination and Assessment Center.

Wells, G. (1986). *The meaning makers: Children learning language and using language to learn.* Portsmouth, NH: Heinemann.

CHAPTER 2

English as a Second Language Learners

Limited English proficient (LEP) students are those individuals who have a primary language other than English and who are learning English as a second or foreign language. In the United States, they are usually immigrants from other countries who have adopted the United States as their second home, or they may have been born in the United States and raised in a non-English environment in which their parents may have little understanding of English. Also, chances are they have been living in the country for only a short period of time. Another group of ESL students are those who are learning English in countries where English is not the language of the country, and English becomes a foreign or second language. Thus, there is a variety of ESL learners. Second language learners vary not only in terms of location and purpose for learning English but in terms of individual differences. This chapter addresses those individual differences that make some second language learners more successful than others and require language educators to provide an instructional environment that meets those individual differences.

Individual Learners' Differences

Variety in second language acquisition is influenced by individual differences in the way learners learn a second language and the way they use their language knowledge. Learning is affected by many conditions both internal and external to learners. There is, in any group, a wide range of individual differences in styles, strategies, and pace of learning. Learners are not always conscious of these components, yet their influence or involvement can determine one's success.   Aptitude, personality, attitude and motivation, and cognitive/learning style are factors among others, impacting on a learner's second language acquisition. These factors influence the rate and success of second language acquisition and have social, cognitive, and affective implications. Social aspects are external to the learner and concern the relationship between learners and native speakers of the second language and also between the learners and other speakers of their own language. Cognitive and affective aspects are internal to learners.   Cognitive factors concern the nature of the conceptual strategies used by learners while affective factors concern the emotional responses related to the attempts to learn the second language.

Aptitude

Aptitude refers to the special ability involved in language learning. It is usually defined in terms of the tests that have been used to measure it (Ellis, 1990). The term was originally created by John Carroll, a psychologist who developed a test called *The Language Aptitude Test* (LAT) to predict performance of students in foreign language learning (Carroll, 1967).   Carroll and Sapor (1959) identified three major components of aptitude: (a) phonetic coding ability (ability to perceive and memorize new sounds, (b) grammatical sensitivity (the individual's ability to demonstrate awareness of the syntactical patterning of sentences of a language), and (c) inductive ability (ability to notice and identify similarities and differences in both grammatical form and meaning).   Pimleurs (1966) also has defined language aptitude.   His definition includes: (a) verbal intelligence (familiarity with words, and ability to reason analytically about verbal materials), (b) motivation to learn the language, and (c) auditory ability. The structural measures that have been used to obtain aptitude scores involve mainly the ability to learn sound and grammar and have been created primarily for use with English-speaking learners of foreign languages, and not with native speakers of non-English languages.

Although the influence of aptitude on second language acquisition cannot be traced accurately, Gardner (1980) indicated that aptitude is a major factor determining the level of success of classroom language learning.   He correlated Canadian school children's scores on the *Modern Language Aptitude Test* and their grade levels in French.

Gardner found a strong relationship between aptitude and proficiency. Other authorities have discussed the similarities and differences between aptitude and intelligence. Oller and Perkins (1978), among others, have disputed the idea of a separate, purely linguistic ability. They have argued that general intelligence and ability to use one's native language in language tests are essentially the same.

Limited English proficient individuals come with different oral bases, different literacy traditions, different writing systems, different concepts of sound-symbol relations and different modes of normal discourse along with strong patterns, and different levels of development in their primary languages. What role does the "special ability" involved in language learning play? Aptitude may be an important factor in the rate of development, particularly in formal classroom ESL instruction (Ellis, 1990; Krashen, 1981a). Those ESL students with a "talent" for formal instruction are likely to learn more rapidly. Ellis (1990) summarized this important question by saying: "aptitude may be age-related. It may develop along with the general ability for abstract thinking. Aptitude is also likely to affect ultimate success in second language acquisition, particularly if this is measured by formal tests of linguistic competence" (p. 113).

Personality

Personality refers to a number of personal traits in the individual. Although the available research does not show a clearly defined effect of personality on second language learning in general, it has been indicated to play a major role in the acquisition of communicative competence. It has been said that extroverted learners learn more rapidly and are more successful than introverted learners because extroverted learners will find it easier to make contact with other speakers of the target language (Ellis, 1990; Krashen, 1981b). Another element mentioned that emphasizes personal dispositions of individuals is social skills involved in second language acquisition. Fillmore's study (1979) concluded that social skills of individuals controlled the amount of exposure to the second language. Speaking of the most successful learners in her study, Fillmore says: "To learn a language rapidly, it is perhaps most necessary to identify with the people who speak it...Nora...not only wanted to be around English speakers, she wanted to be *like* them, and therefore, she adopted their way of talking" (Fillmore, 1979, p. 227). Also, "The children...were more or less equally endowed with the intellectual capacity to learn a new language but they were differently disposed to take the necessary steps to insure the learning of the second language" (p. 227).

Although Strong (1983) did not agree with Fillmore's idea that a key to acquiring a second language centers on a motivation to become part of the world of the target language group, he stated that what contributed to the acquisition of English were those personality traits that controlled the quality of interaction in the second language. Strong concluded that:

> The issue is, I propose, not that better learners are getting more input than their peers, but rather that they are making more active use of the English they are exposed to...This active use, reflected by traits of talkativeness and responsiveness, might involve not only better concentration or a greater tendency to process what they hear, but also a facility for keeping conversations going. (pp. 251-252)

Inhibition is another personality trait that has been mentioned in the literature as negatively affecting second language acquisition. Krashen (1981) indicated that inhibition produces egocentrism which in turn leads to increased self-consciousness. In spite of scarcity of research in the role of personality in second language acquisition, there is a general conviction that it is a very important variable (Naiman, Fröhlich, Stern, and Todesco, 1978; Krashen, 1981b). Naiman, Fröhlich, Stern and Todesco said: "Certain personality and cognitive style factors are related to success in language learning" (p. 100). Traits relating to self-confidence (lack of anxiety, outgoing personality, self-esteem) are predicted to relate to second language acquisition (Brown, 1977; Krashen, 1981a, 1981b).

Attitude and Motivation

Attitude has been defined as the set of beliefs that learners hold toward members of the target language group and toward their own culture (Brown, 1981) or as the persistence shown by language learners in striving for a goal (Gardner and Lambert, 1972). Gardner and Lambert said: "It was our hunch that an integrative orientation would sustain better the long-term motivation needed for the very demanding task of second-language learning..." (p. 131). And, perhaps then the knack for languages lies in the profile of abilities or aptitudes from person to person. They also stressed that learning takes place when the learner wants something, notices something, does something, and receives something" (p. 134). Stern (1983) classified attitudes in three types: (a) attitudes toward the community and people who speak the second language, (b) attitudes toward learning the target language, and (c) attitudes toward languages and language learning in general. Factors that encourage intake and motivational variables have been found to be related to second language acquisition (Krashen, 1981). These factors encourage learners to communicate with speakers of the second language and obtain the necessary input or intake for language acquisition (orientation of the learner toward the speakers of the target language).

Oller, Hudson, and Liu (1977) conducted a study to investigate the relation between various measures of attitudes toward self, the native language group, the target language group, reasons for learning English as a second language, reasons for traveling to the United States and attaining proficiency in ESL. The subjects were 44 Chinese-speaking foreign students primarily studying at the graduate level in the United States. It was hypothesized that positive attitudes, especially positive attitudes toward the target language group, would correspond to higher attainment in the target language, and similarly negative attitudes, especially toward the target language group, would correspond to lower attainment in the target language. The researchers found that, in general, attitudes toward self and the native language group– as well as attitudes toward the target language group were positively correlated with attained proficiency in ESL. However, the relationship between reasons for studying ESL, such as traveling to the United States and attained proficiency, was contrary to previous predictions. For instance, there was a significant negative correlation between desire to stay in the United States permanently and attained ESL proficiency. Gardner and Lambert (1972) suggested that attitudes are related to motivation by serving as supports of learners' overall orientation.

Motivation is one of the more complex issues of second language acquisition. Gardner and Lambert (1972) defined motivation in terms of the second language learners' overall goal or orientation. Research on motivation has focused on Gardner's (1980, 1985) distinction between integrative (desire to learn a language stemming from a positive attitude toward a community of its speakers) and instrumental (desire to learn a language in order to attain certain career, educational or financial goals) orientations of second language learners. When the practical value of second language proficiency is high, and frequent use of the language necessary, instrumental motivation is a powerful predictor of second language acquisition (Gardner & Lambert, 1972). They have found that a high level of students' drive to acquire the language of a valued second language community, combined with inquisitiveness and interest in the group, should underlie the motivation needed to master a second language. Later on, Gardner (1988) added that: "...integratively-motivated students tend to be more active in learning the language and tend to be more proficient in a second language" (p. 113). Also, learners who are instrumentally motivated are not necessarily interested in the language or the culture of the target language group; their interest is personal satisfaction and the benefits that might be derived from learning the second language. Favorable attitudes to learn the second language seem to correlate highly with measures of achievement (Gardner, 1985; Gardner & Lambert, 1972).

Motivation has been called the most important variable in foreign language learning. Of the possible motivators, the desire for integration with the culture of the speakers of the language correlates most highly with learning success. McNamara (1973) argued that need to communicate, more than attitude, provides the most tangible kind of motivation. He contended that lack of communicative purpose in the language classroom underlies students' poor language competence, rather than poor attitudes. An important component involved in motivation is having a goal to learn the language (Gardner, 1985). It appears that motivation is a powerful factor in second language acquisition and that attitudes contribute to the degree of second language acquisition. But Hakuta (1986) posed an interesting question: "How do we know that positive attitudes result in more second language learning, rather than that more second language learning results in more positive attitudes?" (p. 159). There is no clear answer to this question. Perhaps, it may be both.

Cognitive/Learning Style

Learning style refers to an individual's consistent and rather enduring preferences, vis a vis, general characteristics of intellectual functioning and personality. Examples of learning styles may include:

tolerance of ambiguity; more or less reflective, or impulsive; less field dependent/independent, oriented – more or less toward imagery; more or less holistic, analytical or logical. There are a number of hypotheses about the role of each of these terms in second language acquisition. One of the most interesting assumptions is the suggestion that field dependence will prove most facilitative in naturalistic second language acquisition, but field independence will lead to greater success in classroom learning. Ellis (1990) has defined these two terms based on general characteristics. Characteristics of "field dependent individuals," include among others: (a) reliance on external frame of reference in processing information, (b) perception of a field as a whole, (c) self-view derived from others, and (d) greater skill in interpersonal/social relationships. Field independent individuals are characterized as: (a) reliance on internal frame of reference in processing information, (b) perceives field in terms of its component parts, (c) sense of separate identity, and (d) less skilled in interpersonal/social relationships. The reasoning is that the more social skills learners have, the greater their contact with the target language native speakers, and the more input they receive. On the other hand, in classroom learning, the ability to analyze formal rules is very important. This distinction does not mean that one learning style is better than the other in facilitating second language acquisition. It is assumed that "field independent learners" will perform some tasks more effectively than "field dependent learners," and vice versa. Authorities have found different types of results in learners acquiring a second language. For example, Naiman et al. (1978) found some evidence to show that learners produce different kinds of errors, related to their cognitive style. They found that analytic learners were more likely to omit small items than whole phrases in sentence imitation, while holistic learners were more likely to do the opposite.

Other Variables

Second language learners represent a wide range of language variations with varying levels of literacy and proficiency in the first as well as in the second language. There are students who show linguistic deficiencies relative to their age in both the primary and the second language. Other students come to the ESL classroom with the ability to analyze and reformulate material. Also, the organization and analysis of knowledge may differ from culture to culture. These factors, therefore, play an important role in planning for the development of linguistic and cognitive skills in English. All ESL students bring a lifetime of language strengths to the learning situation. Among the most significant are: (a) skills in their first (native) language, which encompass listening, speaking, reading and writing; (b) broad, biculturally based cognitive and affective experiences that enable them to survive successfully in "two worlds"; (c) social intelligence–that is–"personal psychological insight and the capacity for empathy." Concepts already learned in the LEP students' native language can be transferred into English and developed as students apply them to many second language activities. They have acquired valuable conceptualization of the world around them in their native language. All these ideas and concepts which have been developed in the native language stand for a powerful language strength during the second language acquisition process. Second language learners have different experiences and background knowledge which in turn will affect their conceptualization of the world and their personal psychological insights. Furthermore, individuals in a second language classroom will have different feelings and reactions to various situations which they will encounter.

In addition to these skills, LEP students possess a broad cultural background, as well as a global conceptual view that aid them in comprehending the semantics of English. The LEP students are also influenced by their immediate environment. In terms of age, older children and adolescents learn better than younger children in acquiring a second language in a natural environment (Ervin-Trip, 1974; Krashen, Long & Scarcella, 1982; McLaughlin, 1984). In this respect, social and psychological maturity play crucial roles in LEP students' language development. Younger children require the formal classroom environment, and yet, at the same time, they may be able to acquire a second language while still learning their first one.

Limited English proficient students can share their own ideas and experiences that are rich in information concerning their customs, languages, and perceptions of the world. All the experiences and knowledge LEP students have encountered can be used as a useful resource to plan and structure second language learning activities. Using experiences and concepts already acquired makes the second language learning experience more interesting and meaningful because students are able to relate and understand the concepts being used. English as a second language educators must take advantage of the language and cultural strengths and of the valuable knowledge limited English proficient students bring to the classroom. Using the student's language and cultural strengths to plan learning and teaching strategies strengthens the individual's self-concept and promotes a close working relationship between teacher and learner.

Age and Second Language Acquisition: Children/Adults Differences

Who are "better" in second language acquisition, children or adults? Another question that has arisen is whether adults learn a second language in the same way as children. A common sense approach may indicate that since children and adults are not the same, there is a need to recognize their differences in second language acquisition. The notion that it is better to learn a second language early rather than late is a common one. For years, there was the belief that children, especially young children, are better able to learn a second language than adults. The theory indicated that children acquire language "naturally" and without effort, that they learn faster or better than adults. It accompanies the idea that native-like mastery of phonology, and adeptness in imitation, can only be expressed by those who learn the target language early.

The belief in the superiority of children over adults in second language learning is strong, and probably results from the common observation that children living in a foreign country seem rapidly to achieve native-like fluency in the target language, while their parents may lag far behind. The implication is that children have a biological predisposition for language learning which is perhaps related to brain plasticity and imprinting. The brain plasticity theory suggests that the child's brain has a cellular receptivity to language acquisition. This receptivity may be a function of cellular plasticity or elasticity which is controlled by a sort of biological clock (Penfield & Roberts, 1959; Lenneberg, 1967). With age this biology changes the cellular plasticity, which reduces the organic capacity to learn language. It was generally thought that the left hemisphere of the brain became lateralized or specialized for language function at the age of two, and this lateralization process continued until puberty. After puberty, the brain lost plasticity and it became extremely difficult to acquire language. An inference frequently drawn from the critical period hypothesis was that younger children learn languages better than older ones. Lenneberg (1967), with whom the notion of an age limitation in language acquisition is most often associated, constructed an argument that there exists a period lasting roughly from the second to the tenth or twelfth year during which the child is able to fully exploit its capacity to acquire its native language. Lenneberg also suggested that this special state of receptivity extends to non-native languages as well and that the drop-off in acquisition efficiency around age 10 affects the ability to learn any natural language completely.

Recent research, however, indicates that there is no direct evidence that children have a special learning capacity which is absent in adults (Harley, 1986). Also, although the left brain is specialized for language function to a great extent, no clear evidence exists yet on when lateralization for language is complete. Krashen (1973) believed that lateralization occurs at four or five years of age and not at puberty and that there may be different critical periods for different abilities, which in turn determine how completely one can acquire some aspects of language.   Walsh and Diller (1981) state that there is "overwhelming evidence" which shows that language learning ability does not deteriorate with age. In fact, although children do acquire better pronunciation than adults, "As people grow older and cognitively more mature, their increasing higher order cortical functions allow them to do more than they could before" (p. 18). Littlewood (1984) observes that one difficulty in comparing younger learners with older ones is that younger ones generally have better learning conditions; more time, attention, communicative need, and opportunities for using the target language.   He says that some researchers have found that where opportunities are equalized, older learners seem to learn more quickly and efficiently.   It appears that factors such as motivation, greater cognitive maturity, more developed native language skills and a greater need to communicate orally contribute to adults' or older children's superior performance in the second language.

Related to the question of age, a distinction is made between "formal" and "informal" language instruction.   Krashen (1981b) suggests that children "acquire" or informally "pick up" language and adults "learn" formally through study, as well as informally picking it up. In a study of adult language learning, Krashen (1976) cited Fathman (1975) who investigated the relationship between certain aspects of the second language acquisition process and age. An oral production test was developed to produce standard English morphology and syntax. The test was administered to approximately 200 children (ages 6-15) who were learning English as a second language in American public schools. The results of this testing were used to examine the relationship between age and the rate of acquisition of certain English grammatical structures, and the order of acquisition of these grammatical structures. The results indicated that there was some relationship between age and the rate of learning. Among children exposed to English the same amounts of time, the older children scored higher on the morphology and syntax sub-tests, whereas the younger children received higher rating in phonology. There were, however, no major differences observed in the order in which children of different ages learned to produce the structures included in the test. The results suggest that there is a difference in the rate of learning of English morphology, syntax, and phonology based upon differences in age, but that the order of acquisition in second language learning does not change with age.

Pronunciation or "accent" is the aspect of second language acquisition most often believed to be rather closely age-related. Oyama (1982), in a study of sensitive period and comprehension of speech, found that those second language learners who began learning English by age 10 tended to resemble native speakers in their ability to deal with marked speech, those who began in early adolescence diverged from native levels, and those who began after mid-adolescence showed markedly lower average comprehension scores. Oyama (1982) concluded that: "...human beings are better able to analyze, integrate and fully utilize a new language if they approach it early in life than if they do so after the early trend" (p. 45).

Most of the literature on child and adult differences in second language acquisition points to similarities and differences related to age, rate, and attainment. Hakuta (1986) summarized related studies and concluded that those that learn a second language in childhood (before puberty) are more successful than those who acquire it as adults. This is not just for accent (Asher & Garcia, 1969), but for grammar as well. However, Hakuta cited studies that suggest an advantage for the older learner. Krashen (1982) cited a study by

Krashen, Long and Scarcella (1979) that summarized those differences and similarities. These are:

1. Adults proceed through the early stages of syntactic and morphological development faster than children (where time and exposure are held constant).
2. Older children acquire faster than younger children (again in the early stages of syntactic and morphological development where time and exposure are held constant).
3. Acquirers who begin with natural exposure to second languages during childhood generally achieve higher second language proficiency than those beginning as adults (pp. 202).

The available evidence suggests that age does not alter the route of second language acquisition. Learners appear to process linguistic data in the same way, irrespective of how old they are. However, rate and success appear to be influenced by age of the learner. Adults acquire primary levels more rapidly, perhaps because of their greater cognitive abilities. Age is a factor in second language acquisition when it comes to morphology and syntax. In pronunciation, younger learners do better perhaps because they are strongly motivated to be part of the community which speaks the second language (Hakuta, 1986; Ellis, 1990; Krashen, 1981b; 1982). Most researchers argue that the greater the exposure to the second language, the more native-like language proficiency. Children will achieve more overall communicative fluency because they are likely to receive more years of exposure to the second language and their interaction with peer groups who speak the target language. Krashen (1981b) explained this aspect by explaining that pronunciation runs deeper into the center of the student's personality than any other aspect of language.

Adults, and older children in general, initially acquire the second language faster than younger children. Krashen (1981b) argued that older is better for rate of acquisition, but child second language acquirers will usually be superior in terms of ultimate attainment. In order for an adult to "pick up" a language, the adult has to use it regularly and use it in meaningful situations. Formal language classes are more effective than mere informal exposure (i.e., living in the second language environment but making no real attempt to communicate in the second language regularly). Formal language classes and having a meaningful informal exposure to the second language both contribute to language learning.

The Role of the First Language

It is a popular belief that second language acquisition is strongly influenced by a learner's first language. There is disagreement among researchers about the extent and nature of the role of first language in second language acquisition. The role of first language was first studied in terms of the "transfer" theory, in which errors in second language acquisition were seen as the result of interference from the first language. The contrastive analysis movement studied the interfering effects or areas of difficulties between the native languages and the second language. Teaching would provide practice to eliminate these errors. Several years later, this theory was modified to identify similarities in the first and second language. More recently, the role of first language in communicative tasks has begun to emerge. Contrastive pragmatics analyzes the role of first language in the knowledge of speakers dealing with language in conversations, including relevant non-verbal aspects of language use.

The first language is a resource ESL students use consciously or subconsciously to help them "shift the L2 data and the input and to perform as best as they can in L2" (Ellis, 1990; p. 40). How a student uses the first/primary language as a resource depends on a series of factors related to the formal and pragmatic features of the first and second language and the learner's stage of development. Transferability of skills from one language to another reappears to play a critical role in second language acquisition. Vygotsky (1962) maintained that there are two types of knowledge: spontaneous knowledge, which refers to familiar, everyday concepts, and scientific knowledge, which encompasses formal, school-learned concepts. Once a number of scientific concepts are mastered, the awareness of their development spreads in everyday concepts. By the age of 10, children use both scientific and spontaneous concepts intelligently. Vygotsky (1962) stated that:

> Success in learning a foreign language is contingent on a certain degree of maturity in the native language. The child can transfer to

the new language the system of meanings he already possesses in his own. (p. 110)

Baetens-Beardsmore (1986) stated that there is a unified underlying system, sharing rules and linguistic characteristics. There exists a transfer of universal linguistic characteristics and specific knowledge acquired from one language to another. The influence of the first language is likely to be more evident in second language phonology, especially in the accent. This is not to say that it has a negative influence. On the contrary, it helps second language learners by providing a linguistic and cognitive framework, especially at the beginning stage. It has been hypothesized that as the learners' proficiency grows in the second language, the influence of the first language is less powerful.

The Good Language Learner

There has been a number of attempts to describe characteristics of the "good language learner." Rubin (1975) has listed seven of them. According to Rubin, the good language learner (a) is a willing and accurate guesser, (b) desires to communicate, or to learn from communication, (c) is uninhibited and willing to appear foolish, (d) attends to form, looks for patterns in language, (e) practices, (f) monitors his own speech and that of others, and (g) attends to meaning. Other characteristics could be added to this list. For example, studies suggest that perceived aptitude is not as important to successful language learning as persistence and a willingness to adapt to varied learning situations (Naiman et al., 1978). The good language learner is willing to put in the time to develop language. Researchers have found that the amount of time a learner spends acquiring the second language is a major determinant in his or her success (Cumming, 1989). Moreover, the second language learner cannot be considered knowledgeable unless he or she knows essential facts about the second culture and understands the behavior of its members (Hammerly, 1985). Thus, it stands to reason that good language learners will seek to acquire this knowledge as well.

The above characteristics to some extent reflect the social, cognitive, and affective factors that have been found important in second language acquisition. Some of these characteristics relate to individuals' cognitive and linguistic strengths, while others relate to the learning strategies they employ. In most cases, second language learners cope with three major learning problems: the discrepancy between the primary and second language, the code communication dilemma, and the choice between rational and intuitive learning (Reiss, 1985). In dealing with these problems, good strategy is vitally important. According to Littlewood (1984), successful second language learners make use of a wide variety of strategies which demonstrate an active involvement with learning. Certain strategies are important at the initial learning stage during the learning process. Consequently, Rubin (1980) developed 10 learning process strategies which are used by good language learners: (a) a personal, positive learning style, (b) an active approach to the learning task, (c) a tolerant and ongoing approach to the target language and empathy with its speakers, (d) technical know-how about how to tackle a language, (e) tactical use of experimentation and planning with the object of developing the new language into an ordered system and of revising this system progressively, (f) an on-going search for meaning, (g) a willingness to practice, (h) a willingness to use the language in real communication, (i) self-monitoring and critical sensitivity to language use, and (j) developing the target language more and more as a separate reference system and learning to think in it. These strategies, although impressive, lack sufficient empirical data as to their success.

Krashen (1981b) summarized the qualities of good language learners by saying that the good language learner is an acquirer, who first of all is able to obtain sufficient intake in the second language and, second, has a low affective filter to enable him to utilize the input for language acquisition. Good language learners find opportunities to learn and practice the target language in both formal and informal situations, and they use learning as a supplement to acquisition. They self-monitor but do not let it get in the way of communicating (Krashen, 1981a). Naiman, Fröhlich, Stern, and Todesco (1978) reinforce this point by saying:

> All forms of language teaching could be greatly improved if we had
> a better understanding of the language learner and of the language
> process itself" (p. 1). Also, Certain personality and cognitive style

factors are related to success in language learning. The present study identified two such factors as important: tolerance of ambiguity and field independence. (p. 100)

References

Asher, J. & Garcia, G. (1969). The optimal age to learn a foreign language. *Modern Language Journal, 38*, 334-41.

Baetens-Beardsmore, H. (1986). *Bilingualism: Basic principles.* Avon, England: Multilingual Matters.

Brown, H. (1977). Introduction. In C. Snow and C. Ferguson (Eds.), *Talking to children: Language input and acquisition.* Cambridge, MA: Cambridge University Press.

Brown, H. (1981). Affective factors in second language learning. In J. Alatis, H. Altman & P. M. Alatis (Eds.), *The second language classroom: Directions for the 1980's* (pp. 111-129). New York: Oxford University Press.

Carroll, J. & Sapor, S. (1959). *Modern language aptitude test (MLAT).* New York: Psychological Corporation.

Carroll, J. (1967). Foreign language proficiency levels attained by language majors near graduation from college. *Foreign Language Annuals, 1* (2), 131-151.

Cumming, A. (1989). Writing expertise and second language proficiency. *Language Learning, 39* (1), 81-141.

Ellis, R. (1990). *Understanding second language acquisition.* Oxford, England: Oxford University Press.

Ervin-Trip, S. M. (1974). Is second language learning like the first? *TESOL Quarterly, 8*(2), 111-127.

Fathman, A. (1975). The relationship between age and second language productive ability. *Language Learning, 25,* 245-266.

Fillmore, W. (1979). Individual differences in second language acquisition. In C. Fillmore, D. Kempler & W. S. Y. Wang (Eds.), *Individual differences in language ability and language behavior* (pp. 203-228). New York: Academic Press.

Gardner, R. & Lambert, W. (1972). *Attitudes and motivation in second language learning.* Rowley, MA: Newbury House.

Gardner, R. (1980). On the validity of affective variables in second language acquisition. Conceptual, contextual and statistical considerations. *Language Learning, 30,* 255-270.

Gardner, R. C. (1985). *Social psychology and second language learning: The role of attitudes and motivation.* Great Britain: Edward Arnold .

Gardner, R. C. (1988). The socio-educational model of second language learning: Assumptions, findings and issues. *Language Learning, 38*(1), 101-128.

Hakuta, K. (1986). *Mirror of language.* New York: Basic Books.

Hammerly, H. (1985). *An integrated theory of language teaching.* Blaine, WA: Second Language Publications.

Harley, B. (1986). *Age in second language acquisition.* Avon, England. Multilingual Matters.

Krashen, S. (1973). Lateralization, language learning and the critical period. Some new evidence. *Language Learning, 23,* 63-74.

Krashen, S. D. (1976). Formal and informal linguistic environments in language learning and language acquisition. *TESOL Quarterly,* 157-168.

Krashen, S. D. (1981a). Aptitude and attitude in relation to second language acquisition and learning. In K. C. Diller (Ed.), *Individual differences and universals in language learning aptitude* (pp. 155-175). Rowley, MA: Newbury House.

Krashen, S. D. (1981b). *Second language acquisition and second language learning.* Oxford: Pergamon.

Krashen, S. D. (1982). Accounting for child/adult differences in second language rate and attainment. In S. D. Krashen, R. C. Scarcella & M. H. Long. *Child-Adult differences in second language acquisition* (pp. 202-226). Rowley, MA: Newbury House.

Krashen, S. D., Long, M. & Scarcella, R. (1979). Age, rate and eventual attainment in second language acquisition. *TESOL Quarterly, 13*, 573-582.

Krashen, S. D., Long, M. H. & Scarcella, R. C. (1982). Age, rate and eventual attainment in second language acquisition. In S. D. Krashen, R. C. Scarcella, & M. H. Long (Eds.), *Issues in second language research* (pp. 161-172). Rowley, MA: Newbury House.

Lenneberg, E. (1967). *Biological foundations of language.* New York: Wiley & Sons.

Littlewood, W. (1984). *Foreign second language learning.* New York: Cambridge University Press.

MacLaughlin, B. (1984). *Second language acquisition in childhood.* Hillsdale, NJ: Lawrence Erlbaum Associates.

McNamara, J. (1973). Attitudes and learning a second language. In R. W. Shuy & R. W. Rasold (Eds.), *Language attitudes: Current trends and prospects* (pp. 36-40). Washington, DC: Georgetown University Press.

Naiman, N., Fröhlich, H., Stern, H. & Todesco, A. (1978). *The good language learner*. Toronto, Ontario: Ontario Institute for Studies in Education.

Oller, J. & Perkins, K. (1978). A further comment on language proficiency as a source of variance in certain affective measures. *Language Learning, 28*(2), 417-423.

Oller, J. W., Hudson, A. J. & Liu, P. F. (1977). Attitudes and attained proficiency in ESL: A sociolinguistic study of native speakers of Chinese in the United States. *Language Learning, 27*, 1-27.

Oyama, S. (1982). The sensitive period and comprehension of speech. In S. D. Krashen, R. C. Scarcella & M. H. Long (Eds.), *Child-adult differences in second language acquisition* (pp. 39-51). Rowley, MA: Newbury House.

Penfield, W. & Roberts, L. (1959). *Speech and brain mechanism*. New York: Atheneum Press.

Pimleurs, P. (1966). *Pinsleur Language Aptitude Battery (PLAB)*. New York: Harcout Brace Jovanovich.

Reiss, M. A. (1985). The good language learner: Another look. *The Canadian Modern Language Review*, 41(3), 510-523.

Rubin, J. (1975). What the "good language learner" can teach us. *TESOL Quarterly*, 9(1), 41-51.

Stern, H. (1983). *Fundamental concepts of language teaching*. Oxford: Oxford University Press.

Stern, H. H. (1975). What can we learn from the good language learner? *The Canadian Modern Language Review*, 31 (4), 304-18.

Strong, M. (1983). Social styles and the second language acquisition of Spanish speaking kindergardeners. *TESOL Quarterly, 17*(2), 241-258.

Vygotsky, L. S. (1962). *Thought and language.*   Cambridge, MA: MIT Press.

Walsh, T. M. & Diller, K. C. (1981).   Neurolinguistic considerations on the optimum age for second langauge learning.   In K. C. Diller (Ed.), *Individual differences & universals in language learning aptitude* (pp. 3-21).   Rowley, MA: Newbury House.

CHAPTER 3

Cultural Diversity in the ESL Classroom

Culturally diverse groups enrich the United States and provide opportunities for people to understand differences. This leads eventually to high levels of acceptance and respect for all people. Increasing numbers of children from language minority backgrounds are entering United States schools who have little or no proficiency in the English language. While Spanish is the predominant first language of many LEP children in the United States, an increasing number are entering the schools speaking Chinese, Korean, Haitian/Creole, Lao, Vietnamese, and/or Russian. The increasing number of ethnically, linguistically, and economically diverse children in public school classrooms has underscored tremendously the striking differences in family structure, lifestyle, language and learning styles together. The increasing linguistic and cultural diversity of the school population challenges educators, especially those directly involved in teaching LEP children to understand different values, customs, and traditions and to provide them with responsive learning experiences. Ethnic and linguistic groups differ in their values, mores, and their interaction of experiences. Language differences are probably the most obvious problem which must be overcome when crossing cultural groups because language reflects the thought processes of a culture. Attitudes toward the target language, the difficulties in learning the target language, as well as its relation to learning are important language variables. People of different societies think differently about language, value it differently, acquire it through different social mechanisms, and use it in different situations. This chapter presents an overview of the socio-cultural elements to consider in providing ESL instruction to students for whom English is a second or foreign language.

53

Cultural Influences in Second Language Learning

Different socio-cultural groups perceive the world in very different terms. Culture is socially constructed by human beings in interaction with one another. Cultural ideas and understandings are shared by a group of people who recognize the knowledge, attitudes, and values of one another. Cushner, McClelland & Safford's, (1992) definition of culture includes several components. They defined culture as follows:

> Culture as a socially constructed and dynamic phenomenon; culture
> as shared by a group that decides through a process of interaction
> what ideas, attitudes, meanings and hierarchy of values belong to
> that group; and culture, as a set of ideas that is passed on to the
> young as a means of nourishing the next generation. (p. 20)

Thus, culture includes institutions, language, values, religion, ideals, habits of thinking, artistic expressions, and patterns of social and interpersonal relationships (Lum, 1986). The melting pot, once thought of as a means of erasing cultural differences, obviously does not assimilate differences and should not be viewed as a means of achieving equality among individuals of different cultural backgrounds. The "salad bowl" perspective, in which all people live together yet hold on to their cultural backgrounds, is a more realistic point of view (McCormick, 1984).

All learning is social (Vygotsky, 1962) and reinforcement and feedback are important components of learning. Learning appears to be characterized by an active, self-paced rhythm in which learners engage content by generating, analyzing, and ordering meanings that appear important to their world of understanding. And this world of understanding is culturally determined. Every word and every expression that people use to get meaning from their environment has a cultural dimension. Culture is the means by which a community communicates and learns from each other. Communication and learning take place when people commonly agree upon a set of meanings in their interactions with each other. Speakers of a language share not only the vocabulary and structure of the language, but they also share the perceptions of reality represented by that vocabulary and structure. Shared values and beliefs create the traditions and social structures that bind a community together and are expressed in their language. Language is a tool of the society that employs it, and the ways in which it is used reflect the culture of that society. This relationship between language and culture forms an important part of the acquisition of a second language because it involves the way in which members of a culture view the world. Whenever second language is mentioned there is the notion of two cultures, the mainstream culture and the culture that ESL individuals bring to the second learning setting. ESL students are learning between the values of the native culture and the mainstream culture, and they need to make choices to adapt, reject, accept, and select norms and mores to live by in the new country. The mainstream culture holds opinions of ESL students, and they may not always be favorable, since mainstream individuals can value them according to their own ways of thinking. The interactions of the two cultures can cause misunderstanding among ESL and mainstream students. The language of the school includes the more formal and academic spoken and written varieties of language found and used in schools. What children encounter, then, is a mismatch between the language of the home environment and the language of the classroom. It has been said over and over again that language minority students who have a strong foundation of oral and literacy skills in their first language are able to learn English and learn better and more efficiently than those without that foundation. It is this language foundation that enables them to exercise control over the use of the new language.

Understanding a cultural group may not be sufficient in enabling students of that group to succeed. Within that group there are many differences due to several factors such as socioeconomic status, family structure, and educational background. Also, limited English proficient students (LEP) entering schools using only English as a medium of communication display a wide range of abilities and maturation levels, as well as a variety of language experiences and competencies, a diversity of life experiences, and inclination to learn in particular ways that are at least partially rooted in their socialization in the family. For example, among LEP students there is a great diversity of family patterns. A significant group of these students have a family structure of a single parent, often a mother and child or children living in poverty. However, there is another group of LEP learners who enjoy the comfort of two parents–mother and father. A significant group of LEP children live with grandparents, and another LEP group live with foster parents or parents with different sexual orientations. Therefore, every ESL student and family is unique. Also, not all members of a particular cultural/ethnic group share the same experiences or values. Each family interacts in unique ways with the culture and with the environment. ESL students, even when they are from the same ethnic background, may not share identical cultural, social, and linguistic experiences and perspectives. In developing an appropriate ESL program, educators must have an understanding of the socio-cultural environment of their students. ESL educators need to be aware of aspects such as the following:

1. Were LEPs born in the United States, or did they emigrate to the United States? If they emigrated, at what age? For example, Vietnamese students who recently emigrated to the United States bring with them different cultural experiences, differing from Vietnamese students who have been raised in the United States. When the LEP population in the school setting includes students who emigrated to the United States from other countries, it is important to examine factors in the group's past that may have an educational significance. Wars, oppressive regimes, and economic upheavals are among the reasons why many families have left their homeland. Families that have experienced poverty and starvation may have come to the United States in search of employment and better living conditions. ESL learners may have experienced trauma before or during the move to the United States. Finding out about the history of the various cultural ESL students' groups is essential in understanding their problems and their needs.

2. What type of social and economic support does the family of ESL students have? Immigrants tend to settle where there is some form of support available to them. Individuals may live in the local community because of community organizations that support their culture. ESL students whose families are provided assistance from relatives and friends usually have some type of emotional support that facilitates their school's adjustment. But there is another group with no support for whom the ESL and

classroom may be the only support system outside of the immediate family.

3. What is the socioeconomic level of ESL students? Many immigrants and minority groups in the United States are living in extreme poverty. Many ESL students' parents earn less than the minimum wage. Stress, mental and psychological, and various physical problems can occur under extreme conditions of poverty. In many instances the students do not have any type of health insurance.

4. What is the type of family structure and organization of ESL students? The number of people living in the home affects the type of interactions and learning opportunities that ESL students experience. Educators need to be aware that in many ESL students' homes there is no space to do homework, neither is there the quiet and silence needed to study due to overcrowded homes. In cases of extreme poverty, it is not uncommon to find several families living under a single roof. Both parents or the single parent may work long hours and have few opportunities to interact with their children.

5. What are the ESL students' verbal and non-verbal patterns of communication? For example, Chinese students tend to be reluctant to ask questions in class because such behavior is viewed as aggressive and disrespectful in their culture. They may also not volunteer answers during class because their culture expects them to be modest and humble.

6. How do family members of the ESL students view the role of education? A significant group of ESL students come from schools with an authoritarian approach where students are expected to follow rigid rules. Asian students who experienced the structured, lecture method of instruction of Asian countries may feel lost in the American less-structured/open type classroom. It is important to find out about the value placed upon education within the ESL student's family and to identify possible areas of conflict with their own culture.

7. Which are the learning styles represented in the classroom? To some extent learning styles determine a set of characteristics that make the same teaching method effective for some individuals and ineffective to others. Learning styles may include individual responses to the immediate environment (i.e., preference for

quiet or noise), emotionality (i.e., persistence at tasks), social preferences (i.e., working alone or in groups), and specific cognitive orientation (i.e., global versus analytic). Individuals learn how to learn in a particular way. The socialization in a particular culture or ethnic group may have influenced LEP students' style of learning. Students from a particular group may learn how to learn in a specific manner. For example, native Americans may avoid oral discussion situations since their cultural background may have taught them to do so.

Recognizing the diversity in cultural backgrounds is a challenge for many educators today. Many educators assume that culturally and linguistically diverse learners should change cultural values and beliefs to meet the expectations of middle class/American schools. But educators must understand individual learners and their cultural diversity: diversity in learners' families, language, religion, and other significant aspects of their lives. ESL educators are continually challenged to learn what it is like to be a student in a specific culture, how it feels to attend a school that often appears to have strange rules and expectations and how it feels to experience communication problems (Baruth & Manning, 1992).

A Multicultural Learning Environment

The rich cultural diversity of the ESL classroom demands appropriate school and classroom experiences to help learners feel comfortable and able to develop academic and linguistic achievement. The need to understand differences as well as similarities among students will help ESL educators develop appropriate attitudes and perceptions of language minority students, thereby helping them acquire social, academic, and linguistic skills. ESL students require a learning environment in which there is an awareness, understanding, and acceptance of cultural and linguistic differences. This learning environment needs to: (a) develop a culture of the school that reflects multiculturalism, (b) identify ways of working with parents of language minority students, (c) identify mechanisms to improve inter-cultural communication, and (d) practice strategies for effective interaction and learning. The ESL classroom needs to recognize that

LEP students come from a variety of cultural groups and all cultures need to receive the same respect and appreciation.

The Culture of the School

The culture of the school consists of the norms, rules, conditions, social structure, values, beliefs, habits, and experience of life in schools. The culture of the school is maintained by successful parents, teachers, and administrators. Cushner, McClelland and Safford (1992) defined the role of the school as follows: "Students in most schools are expected to learn in- and out-of-context situations through words, symbols, and displays, or at least strive to develop independence and the ability to compete; learn from and be evaluated by adults; obey school personnel in authority; be task oriented; delay gratification of desires to win later rewards; and have a high degree of fluency in the language of the microculture" (p. 105). How can ESL students be successful within the above school system? The school, and not necessarily the students, needs to acquire an awareness of the learners' cultural backgrounds, knowledge of how culture affects motivation and learning, and the skills necessary to work in close interpersonal situations with learners of different cultures and languages. Educators should develop an awareness of learners' cultural backgrounds, their attitudes toward school, and orientation toward achievement. The culture of the school should: (a) develop positive attitudes and values that are conveyed to children, (b) use appropriate curricular and teaching strategies to accommodate different learning styles, (c) foster the development of self-esteem in students, increasing their ability to learn, and (d) model respect and concern for all people (Baruth & Manning, 1992). Effective schools address issues of diversity in their curriculum, emphasizing intercultural competence, teacher expectations, and social relationships in the school and in the community.

Working with the Community

The school is part of the community where it is located. Schools do not exist apart from the other institutions and organizations that comprise the communities in which they operate. Schools are the institutions directly involved in the total educational effort of the community. Teachers and other school personnel can enlist cooperation and help from parents of LEP students. But schools need to be prepared to learn how to ask questions and to ask for help. Many culturally diverse parents may not understand the United States school system and its emphasis on competition and individual achievement. Sometimes not responding to a school call does not necessarily mean that parents do not care.

Parental interest and participation in schools and classrooms have a positive influence on academic achievement. Involved parents help their children in areas of education in which their children need assistance. It has been found that parent involvement in tutoring LEP students is beneficial for children as well as for their parents (Simich-Dudgeon, 1987; Carrasquillo & London, in press).

Another important factor to mention is that for language minority students parental involvement includes other relatives in addition to the mother and father. The grandmother becomes a crucial element in the education of many LEP children. Aunts, uncles, cousins, and older siblings all share the responsibility of helping educate their children.

Improving Intercultural Communication

Educators need to be equipped to understand cultural differences, provide successful student interactions, and be able to teach students from a wide range of backgrounds. Cushner, McClelland and Safford (1992) provide six areas of education to improve inter-cultural communication. They are:

1. Educators should know themselves well. It means identifying the deeply held attitudes, biases, opinions or subjective cultural elements educators carry around. Educators need to be sensitive to the feedback from students, colleagues, and others and should be willing and able to modify their behavior.
2. Educators should use a share code, a shared symbol and communication system when speaking to those who regularly speak another language. Re-phrasing and repetition are recommended for better understanding.
3. Effective communication takes time and demands that people suspend judgment and wait long enough to let other individuals get the meaning of their sentences.
4. Feedback should be welcome. It enables communicators to correct and adjust their messages as needed.

5. Empathy is essential to any communicative effort. One way to develop empathy is that teachers, when speaking, should continuously stop and ask what it might be like to have the experiences of the students whom they are relating to.
6. Avoidance of stereotypes. Although differences are important to be identified, similarities need to be emphasized, especially those characteristics shared by students who attend the same school.

Intercultural communication is also emphasized when providing curricular materials that reflect the culture of the students. These materials should enhance self-concept, maintain interest in classroom learning, and provide models with which culturally different students can relate (Baruth & Manning, 1992; Sleeter & Grant, 1988).

Strategies for Effective Interaction and Learning

Teaching is an activity that involves teachers and learners in interaction. The diversity of the ESL classroom means that ESL educators cannot consider an entire class as a homogeneous group of learners who need the same educational experiences. ESL learners differ not only in terms of social class, geographic location, and family background, but they also differ in values, traditions, and customs. It is the school's responsibility to develop an understanding of each ESL learner and to base teaching/learning experiences on reliable and objective information. ESL classrooms need to emphasize an environment that nurtures students. Cushner, McClelland & Safford (1992) have identified an environment that promotes:

1. *Development of a Positive Self-Image.* Students need to reflect a positive attitude about themselves– that is, in their academic and linguistic ability, and ability to live and learn in the school environment. Cushner, McClelland & Safford (1992) stated: "Environments which invite student participation and where involvement is highly encouraged send the message that students and their concrete experiences are respected and valued and that their contributions are important." (p. 297)
2. *Personal Identity.* Students need to identify who they are in the new and different environment called the "school." For example,

Hispanic ESL students need to see themselves as Hispanic students who are important and active members of the school. Teachers need to create an atmosphere which recognizes individual differences and rewards their contributions to the school environment.

3. *Sense of Pride.* Teachers can help students develop a sense of pride in their own particular ethnic/linguistic group. Teachers need to recognize the contributions (social, economic, political, linguistic) of the cultures represented in the classroom. When students learn about the contributions of their ethnic or religious groups, they are likely to develop pride in their membership in these groups and identify with them.

4. *Sense of Connectedness.* Teachers are responsible for helping students to work with each other rather than perpetuate the individualism and competitiveness that is traditional in many classrooms.

5. *Sense of Confidence.* Students need to develop a sense of confidence in their ability to act, when confronted by prejudice, injustice, or discrimination. ESL students need training in the decision making process in deciding how to act in the schools, in the community, and in the world.

It is imperative that ESL educators understand the school environment's influence on students. The school environment affects the manner in which children perceive themselves, their cultural images, and their learning growth. ESL students need to feel at home, as part of the school family, and they need to be challenged to be successful language and academic learners.

References

Baruth, L. G. & Manning, M. L. (1992). *Multicultural education of children and adolescents.* Needham Heights, MA: Allyn & Bacon.

Carrasquillo, A. & London, C. B. (In press). *Parental involvement in education: A Resource Guide.* New York: Garland.

Cushner, K., McClelland, A. & Safford, P. (1992). *Human diversity in education: An integrative approach.* New York: McGraw-Hill.

Lum, D. (1986). *Social work practice and people of color: A process-stage approach.* Monterrey, CA: Brooks.

McCormick, T. (1984). Multiculturalism: Some principles and issues. *Theory into Practice, 23,* 93-97.

Sleeter, C. E. & Grant, C. A. (1988). *Making choices for multicultural education: Five approaches to race, class and gender.* Columbus, OH: Merrill.

Simich-Dudgeon, C. (1987). Involving limited-English proficient parents as tutors in their children's education. ERIC/CLL. *News Bulletin, 10*(2), 3-4, 7.

Vygotsky, L. S. (1962). *Thought and language.* Cambridge, MA: MIT Press.

CHAPTER 4

The Development of English Language Proficiency

Language proficiency is not a unidimensional construct but a multifaceted modality, consisting of various levels of abilities and domains. Personal, instructional, and linguistic factors influence the rate of acquisition of a second language and the development of different English language skills. This chapter addresses these issues, specifically: (a) the definition of second language proficiency, (b) how might we differentiate between dominance and proficiency in a second language, and (c) what assessment instruments validly examine a student's ability in all areas of second language. The last section of this chapter presents a synopsis of currently available English language proficiency tests.

Second Language Proficiency: A Definition

Second language proficiency is best defined as the learner's overall knowledge of the target language. Also referred to as "competence," proficiency has several components, including grammatical or linguistic competence, sociolinguistic competence, and communicative competence. When the second language learner's language proficiency is measured, it is usually assessed in relation to the native language speaker's proficiency (Canale & Swain, 1980; Harley, Allen, Cummins & Swain, 1990; Swain, 1985).

There are different interpretations of the nature of language proficiency, of how it develops and what it means to be proficient. For example, Chomsky's (1957) view of language learning is cognitively based. He emphasized the innate contributions and abilities of the learner. He focused on a "language acquisition device" which was embedded in the brain to explain why a normal child can acquire language naturally. He asserted that children are born with innate language-learning abilities that take the form of a language acquisition device that proceeds by hypothesis-testing. Consequently, children acquire a language by making hypotheses about the form of the grammar of the language by which they are surrounded. Children then compare their surrounded grammar with their innate knowledge of possible grammars based on the principles of universal grammar. Language use is thus rule-governed behavior that enables speakers to create new utterances that conform to the rules they have internalized. Chomsky's theory of an innate language acquisition device that proceeds by hypothesis-testing had considerable influence on studies of the acquisition of a first language by children, and later influenced the field of second language acquisition and second language proficiency.

One of the current questions in second language acquisition research is if the teaching of a second language is supposed to recreate the kind of situation in which first languages are learned, and if second language learners are supposed to pass through similar stages of development. Krashen (1981) for example, sees (first and second) language acquisition as a process requiring "meaningful interaction in the target language, natural communication, in which speakers are concerned not with the form of their utterances but with the messages they are conveying and understanding" (p. 1). Krashen (1981) as well as Terrell (1981) maintains that through these techniques the innate capacities to acquire a language all individuals possess will be tapped, students will have ample opportunities to test their hypotheses about the nature of the new language, and their interim grammars will be accepted while they are refining their hypothesis through experiences with the language. Thus, language proficiency has different stages and different functions.

Cummins (1980, 1981) has brought together evidence from various studies that have compared language proficiency scores in two languages to argue that there is a "cross-lingual dimension" to language proficiency. According to Cummins there is some common underlying capacity in both languages, and second language proficiency is related to proficiency in the native language of the individual. He believes that the language learner's native language facilitates second language acquisition. McLaughlin (1990) agrees with Cummins when he stated: "...even when the social environment is the same, two children can differ in their acquisition...I believe there is an interdependence between first and second languages in the cognitive/academic domain because experience with one language gives the learner strategies and metacognitive skills that generalize to subsequent languages." (pp. 172, 173)

Cummins (1981) views language proficiency as the ability to use language for both academic purposes and basic communicative tasks. Cummins indicated that there is a strong relationship between language proficiency and academic/cognitive variables across all four language skills of listening, speaking, reading and writing. He has seen two major dimensions of language proficiency: (a) communicative language skills, and (b) academic language skills. Cummins also indicated that there is a consensus that language proficiency cannot meaningfully be broken down into a variety of several components. This position has implications for the assessment of these skills and also the teaching of these skills. There is evidence that some aspects of first language and second language proficiency are interdependent (manifestations of a common underlying proficiency), and that significant relationships would be predicted between communicative activities in different languages which make similar contextual and cognitive demands on the individual (Cummins, 1981). But, not everyone agrees with Cummins' theory, because his definition of language proficiency and literacy implies a test-based interpretation (Hakuta, 1986). The question of what constitutes "language proficiency" and the nature of its cross-lingual dimensions have suggested ways of making second language acquisition and testing more "communicative" on the assumption that a communicative approach better reflects the nature of language proficiency than one that emphasizes the acquisition of discrete language skills. Bachman (1990) and Bachman & Palmer (1982) applied the concept of communicative competence to the field of measurement, expanding the notion of what constitutes linguistic performance, communicative performance, and measures of linguistic and communicative performance. For Bachman and Palmer, background characteristics of language learners and test method influence second language performance.

Authorities such as Day (1981), Hymes (1971), Canale & Swain (1980) and Swain, (1982) indicate that second language learners need to be able to do more than express imposed ideas in correct grammatical form as they struggle to express meanings for which they do not possess the linguistic means. They need also to know the culturally acceptable ways of interacting with other speakers in different situations and in different relationships. Hymes', (1971) theory of communicative competence consists of the interaction of four language components: grammatical, psycholinguistic, sociolinguistic, and probabilistic. The interaction of these four components is necessary for competent communication to take place. Hymes gave emphasis to the importance of context in determining appropriate patterns of behavior, both linguistic and extralinguistic. Later on, Canale (1980), Canale and Swain (1980), and Swain (1985) proposed a view of communicative competence that built on that of Hymes. Their framework included grammatical competence, sociolinguistic competence, discourse competence, and strategic competence. This conceptualization of language provides: "...a broader view of language that includes not just its grammatical aspects, but also the ability to use language appropriately in different contexts and the ability to organize one's thoughts through language." (Harley, Allen, Cummins & Swain, 1990, p. 7)

Giles and Byrne (1982), Krashen (1982), Lambert and Gardner (1972), Snow (1992), and Swain (1985) go beyond this conceptualization, adding a socio-psychological framework. They maintained that the second language learner possesses a "socio-affective filter" which governs the degree of input processed. Lambert and Gardner (1972) have stressed the role of motivation, focusing on specific components of the acculturation framework and the individual's instrumental need to learn the language. Giles and Byrne (1982) draw from Lambert and Gardner's work on the role of motivation in second language acquisition. Giles and Byrne were concerned with how intergroup/interethnic communication is reflective of socio-psychological attitudes; and they concurred with Lambert and Gardner (1972) that motivation is central to second language proficiency. Other authorities have also given emphasis to the socio-psychological aspects of second language proficiency. Brown (1980) has focused on the cultural adaptation, i.e., "the acculturation model," measuring degrees of social and psychological distance between the second language learner and the culture of the target language.

Another view of second language proficiency is represented by Oller (1979) and Oller & Perkins (1980). They claim that there exists a global language proficiency factor. Oller and Perkins (1980) said that many of the bits and pieces of skill and knowledge posited as separate components of language proficiency, intelligence, reading ability, and other aptitudes may be so thoroughly rooted in a single intelligence base that they are indistinguishable. They suggested that one global factor underlies most aspects of linguistic, academic, and intellectual performance. For Oller and Perkins, deficient language proficiency is related to deficient academic achievement. They allow, however, for the possibility that, in addition to the global proficiency factor which represents the central core of language proficiency, there may be unique variances attributable to specific components of language skills. However, there are other authorities who do not accept the idea that there is a close relationship between language proficiency, intelligence, and academic achievement (Labov, 1970). Most authoritics stated that despite the low level of academic development of second language learners their language proficiency is not deficient (Labov, 1970). But there is no adequate theoretical basis for conceptualizing the relationship between language proficiency and academic achievement. Cummins (1981) argued that the difference is found in the fact that Labov and Oller are discussing different dimensions of language proficiency. Oller (global language proficiency) and Labov (sociocultural factors and sociolinguistic factors) affect educational achievement, not language proficiency.

The theories presented in this section serve to indicate that in order to define second language proficiency there is a need to construct a broad definition that includes components of all the above theories. In other words, language proficiency is creative, is innate, is acquired, is developed in natural and meaningful contexts, is social and affective. There is a relationship between language development and thought in the human mind, and there is some common underlying capacity reflected in both languages. An English proficient student is able to use English to ask questions, to understand other speakers and reading materials, to test ideas, and to challenge what is being asked around. All these aspects need to be incorporated in the process of teaching second language learners to become proficient in the target language.

Language Dominance vs. Language Proficiency

Although "dominance" and "proficiency" are used interchangeably, they are not synonymous. MacNamara's (1967) definition of the term "dominance" suggested "competition between two languages," i.e., there is a tendency for one of the languages to be used in preference to the other, from the point of view of the speaker and the listener. Burt and Dulay (1978) distinguished "language proficiency" as the degree to which an individual exhibits control over the use of the rules of a language for one, some, or all of its numerous and diverse aspects, from "language dominance" which is the relative proficiency in comparison with a second or other language. In other words, a person can be proficient in two or more languages, but, relative to the other languages, one language will be the dominant one, and the individual will be "most proficient" and "most dominant" in one or all of the aspects of that language. McCollum (1981) warned that, although it is often assumed, dominance of the target language does not always imply proficiency. She proposed that dominance in the case of bilinguals be determined by measuring proficiency in the two languages. The language receiving the highest rating in the assessment would be considered dominant. But she agrees with prior authorities who have indicated that labeling speakers dominant and/or proficient based on limited information, such as scores of a proficiency test in only one language or in only one mode, often distorts the true profile of the second language learner's ability (Burt & Dulay, 1978; Dulay & Burt, 1980; McCollum, 1981). Back in 1974, Zirkel presented a case for the "alingual" child, that is, a bilingual student who is equally deficient in both languages. He suggested that educators use parallel tests in the two languages as an indication of dominance.

Burt and Dulay (1978) agreed that typical inferential measures of language dominance needed close examination because dominance in one aspect of the language does not necessarily imply dominance in the other aspects of the same language. Quite often, the English phonology of second language LEP learners is strong; however, their vocabulary as a result of school experience and environment may not be so strong. It is imperative, therefore, that English proficiency assessment include other linguistic dimensions to determine language dominance. Dulay and Burt (1980) later use the term "superiority" in place of dominance to avoid confusion. Concerned with the existence of numbers of limited English proficient (LEP) students who were either English-superior (dominant) or equally limited in the two languages, their study found evidence of the importance of collecting home language data in addition to multiple assessment instruments.

Dominance in English may indicate speakers producing meaningful utterances in the target language, but it does not include native-life control of that language. Harley, Allen, Cummins & Swain, (1990) stressed the importance of finding out in which language a learner is more proficient (dominant), if it is academic language as opposed to social language in order to determine in which language the learner should pursue academic study. Citing a study indicating that a disproportionate number of Hispanic children in Texas have been misplaced in learning disabled classes, the authors emphasized the likelihood that a common misconceptualization of proficiency in English may contribute to such erroneous placement. The authors cautioned that educators must arrive at more accurate ways to distinguish between the ways students are able to use language and their innate intelligence or capacity to learn. Clearly, much more research and application of current theory regarding the notion of dominance and proficiency must be incorporated into the educational system.

The Assessment of English Language Proficiency of Limited English/Non English Speakers

An important initiative in the current educational reform movement today deals with the assessment issue. The area of assessment in second language learning, especially for the limited English and the non-English speaker, plays a key role in deciding the educational plan, and quite often, the student's future (Cohen, 1990; Cummins, 1984; Edelsky, Hudelson, Flores, Barkin, Alterweger and Jilbert, 1983; Ramirez, 1984; Snow, 1992). Professionals recognize the need for testing; however, they are often frustrated by the frequent overemphasis on a singular instrument, the misuse or misinterpretation of data, and the lack of authenticity in the measures selected for program use. The current initiative in language assessment has called for holistic, integrative assessment methodology, since language is no longer considered a sum of its parts but a total entity whose subskills need to be assessed holistically. Assessment data may be gathered through the following resources:

1. School records: Referral forms, cumulative record folder, attendance/health records, guidance counselor's report, previous test records, student's work folder containing samples of classwork and homework.
2. Interviews: Formal and informal; parents, teachers, other school personnel, peers.
3. Observations: Classroom, cafeteria, playground, gymnasium.
4. Informal instruments: Checklists, rating scales, cloze procedures, language samples, task analysis, criterion reference tests, and curriculum-based assessment exercises.
5. Normed and standardized tests.

Testing Limited English/Non English Speakers

Language tests are generally used for diagnosis, placement, analysis of achievement, and for measuring proficiency in the target language. Testing plays a significant role in second language teaching and planning. Typically, standardized as well as informal assessment tools are used throughout the educational program. At the beginning of the instructional program, they are utilized to establish readiness during the student's experience with the second language to determine progress, and at the end of instruction to weigh the effectiveness of the intervention (Alderson, Krahnke & Stansfield, 1987; Oller, 1979). Authorities, differing in their theoretical concepts of the nature of second language proficiency, approach testing from specifically different points of view: (a) recognizing language knowledge as a whole, therefore applying global testing to consider general proficiency; (b) focusing on the individual structures of language knowledge, including an analysis of grammatical, syntactical rules and lexical patterns through error analysis; and (c) measuring proficiency via the learner's ability to communicate in contextual situations.

Limited English/non-English speakers are tested frequently in order to assess their degree of English language proficiency and identify the learner's specific English language strengths and weaknesses. In doing so, language proficiency tests should measure discrete linguistic skill areas (phonology, morphology, syntax, vocabulary) as well as integrated language skills (reading, writing, speaking and listening). Dependent on the assessment purpose, examination of these parts may be to the examiner's/examinee's advantage or disadvantage (Burt & Dulay, 1978; Cummins, 1984; Dietrich, Freeman & Crandall, 1979). Snow (1992) stated that proficiency assessment is meaningless unless it is related to the goals of testing. She believes that since language learners usually have a variety of skills in different areas, it is important to assess a learner's skills across domains and tasks. The following aspects have been addressed in assessing LEP students.

Phonology. Oller (1991) defines phonology as a "matter of determining the surface forms or phonemes, syllabus, lexical items, and larger units of structure." Often referred to as pronunciation in educational circles, phonology investigates both the sounds the language uses as well as the rules for their combination. It differs from the study of speech which is defined as a physical or physiological phenomena. Since the sound system is an integral part of any language, the study of pronunciation must form an important part of an ESL program. Burt and Dulay (1978) warned that testing should not confuse differences in pronunciation with difficulties in speech requiring remediation. They maintain that it is not unusual for a second language speaker to retain an accent even when other areas of the second language have achieved a high level of proficiency. Anderson (1981) stated that a prerequisite for testing language proficiency is a knowledge both of the processes of second language acquisition and the research that relates to the phonological interference that often occurs from the speaker's first language.

Morphology. It is the study of the rules that govern the use of minimal meaningful units of a language, which is actually the study of the "architecture of words" (Gleason, 1989; Parker, 1986). Oller (1991) defined the English language's morphology as that system to do with inflections such as marking the plural form of nouns, verb tenses, verb number, and morphemes used to turn an adjective into a verb. Widdowson (1989) suggested that language learners ought to focus on language use, even memorizing meaningful patterns, and analyzing grammar rules to add to and adapt their understanding of and knowledge about language's structures.

Syntax. It refers to the rules by which sentences are constructed, including the architecture of phrases, clauses, and sentences (Gleason, 1989; Parker, 1986). The syntax of English was defined by Oller (1991) as being "concerned with the sequential or simultaneous arrangement of categories of grammar into texts." Burt and Dulay (1978) defined syntax as the system of rules for the arrangement, interrelationship and form of words, phrases, and sentences in a language. Of the various aspects of a particular language, syntax shows the least variation among speakers of the language. There is a relatively stable order of acquisition among language learners of syntax. Burt and Dulay (1978) indicated that syntax seems to be the most suitable and least biased aspect of a language to rely upon in the evaluation of general linguistic proficiency. Although most of the research conducted in the field of child and adult second language acquisition has concentrated on grammatical structures, tests that concentrate on syntax as a language proficiency assessment rely only on the encoded language components of speaking or writing.

Vocabulary. The lexicon includes the store of words an individual knows, as well as the meaning connections between them (Gleason, 1989; Parker, 1986). Vocabulary or "lexicon" was defined by Oller (1991) as comprising those elements in a language that are acquired as whole units such as words, idioms, and phrases. Testing a language learner's vocabulary is one of the traditional ways of assessing verbal ability. However, most of those instruments assume all examinees to have had the same prior experiences. Burt and Dulay (1978) maintained that most vocabulary tests are only appropriate for homogenous groups because vocabulary is so closely associated with a learner's experience. They pointed out, however, that vocabulary development is obviously necessary for linguistic growth; consequently they do recommend testing of vocabulary but with the use of criterion, not norm-referenced tests.

Today's multiplicity of background requires more appropriate measures so that second language proficiency may be assessed fairly, authentically, and appropriately (Cohen, 1990; Cummins, 1984; Oller, 1991; Larsen-Freeman, 1991). In addition to the above discrete language assessment components, integrative testing language approaches have been recommended. Duran (1984) explained that proficiency assessments which employed integrative approaches examine how linguistic skills interact in "naturally occurring segments of language use." These are listening comprehension, speaking, reading, and writing.

Listening and Speaking

Listening is the ability to understand the language of the speaker, comprehend and extract information, and follow the discourse through which the speaker presents the information. Speaking is the ability to use oral languge appropriately and effectively within the classroom and in social interactions. Listening and speaking tests are interdependent. In testing listening and speaking skills, the aim is at measuring the language learner's ability to distinguish phonemes, stress, and intonation as well as producing the words or sentences accurately. Listening tests measure a person's ability to process the information or comprehend a variety of speech signals and lexical and grammatical rules, while speaking tests measure a person's ability to produce languages meaningfully with a certain degree of fluency and proper grammar or vocabulary. A perusal of the English as a second language tests that accompany this pattern will confirm the general impression of those in language development that most of these language tests attend to listening and that these tests generally require the examinee passively to mark a correct answer. There is a general perception that language tests are generally receptive as opposed to productive because, although productive tests of speaking (and writing) are possible, they are not practical in that it is more difficult to establish reliability and overcome subjective impressions in outcomes that require the examinee to produce language in meaningful situations.

The above problem might be remediated by using a communicative approach as proposed by Canale & Swain (1980) and others which includes a four-skill, four-component model. The Canale/Swain design proposed four areas of knowledge in its framework, including: grammatical competence, sociolinguistic competence, discourse competence, and strategic competence. Each competency encompassed "knowledge" of various aspects of the language (Bachman & Palmer, 1982; Canale & Swain, 1980). This model was the foundation for an alternative, more global assessment, which is both integrative and sociolinguistic in its perspective. This form of testing concentrates less on discrete grammatical forms and function and more on holistic language use for natural purposes in realistic contexts.

Reading and Writing

Reading is the ability to comprehend and interpret text at the age- and grade- appropriate level. Writing is the ability to produce written text with content and format fulfilling individual's needs at the age- and grade- appropriate level. Although not always part of ESL proficiency assessment, reading and writing have gained importance in ESL testing due to the emphasis on communicative competence and integrative assessment. Reading is included more often in ESL assessment than writing. Lowe and Stansfield (1988) explained that reading necessitates indirect methods of assessment such as writing or speaking as opposed to direct methods. They further explained that in the foreign service language assessment, the reading test is operationalized in terms of tasks and the degree of understanding that is required for different levels of tasks. For example, at the intermediate level, the examinee must understand main ideas, and at higher levels of proficiency, the examinee must also understand supporting facts, make inferences, and understand analogies.

Writing has never been given great emphasis in language evaluations. New emphasis is currently being placed on composition rather than on transcription. Cumming (1989) explained his construction of a test for writing expertise for second language learners to have been designed to look at three different aspects of writing performance. These are: (a) the qualities of the texts produced; (b) the attention the writer appeared to have devoted to aspects of writing during decision making, and (c) the problem solving behaviors used to control writing processes. He found that as people gain proficiency in their second language, they become better able to perform in writing in their second language. However, he also concluded that greater proficiency in the second language does not entail any qualitative changes in writing strategies.

With regard to the above discussion of listening, speaking, reading, and writing, perhaps the reader will be persuaded that a more integrative approach to language assessment is on the horizon. This new paradigm includes areas of language assessment which have previously been neglected. Writing, for example, has currently received a great deal of discussion in educational circles. Similarly, ESL teachers/specialists and researchers have begun to examine the role of the writing process, as well as writing portfolio assessment in their specific educational programs. There is a call to use communicative tests of the discrete modes of language use: listening, speaking, reading, and writing and that they should not be treated separately and tested separately, but rather be considered as interacting, inseparable, in such contexts as discussion, studying/researching, and corresponding. Other authorities (Carroll, 1980, for example) have recommended the feasibility of "two tier testing". The first tier test would test general usage or "form" and the second tier would test communicative competence in the context and needs of the particular learner. The criteria of any task within a communicative test would include such performance criteria as: (a) the speed at which a task was accomplished; (b) the accuracy with which the test taker incorporated formal structures of the language tested; (c) the appropriateness of the task in terms of the performance being compared with others' performance in a parallel context, and (d) the number of repetitions or hesitations which interfere with communication.

Ellis (1990) reflected the emerging agreement among language-related authorities that instruction as well as assessment of that instruction begin to focus more on genuine communication, while not ignoring the vital structures of language that make that communication possible. He urged that a clear distinction be made among educators between knowledge about language which is fixed or stable and the ability to use that knowledge. He advocates that educators be interested both in how language is acquired and how that knowledge is put to use. Cohen (1990) emphasized that teachers should at all times be aware of how much learning is going on and the effects of what is taught on what is learned. He added the admonition that if teachers are to use standardized, conventional tests, they should also look carefully at what is actually being measured and whether that something coincides with what they want to measure. Teachers should always analyze results and look for who answered what and for what reason. Most educators and researchers would probably agree with Cohen (1990) that paying attention not just to the product of a test but to the process is of great significance if the test is intended to aid classroom instruction and shed light on students' learning. There is a need for continued research and development of assessment tools designed with a global vision of communication, which is appropriate and authentic, focused on the total learner as she/he is engaged in the language process.

English Language Proficiency Exams

Language proficiency tests are used in almost every state in the United States to identify LEP students. The following is a sampling of testing materials currently used in ESL programs. There are many other tests available in the market. This list is only presented with the purpose of making the reader aware of the variety and diversity of second language tests. Most of the tests listed below were taken from Alderson, Krahnke & Stansfield (1987).

Basic English Skills Test. Kenyon, D. & Stansfield, C. W. (1984). Arlington, VA: The Center for Applied Linguistics. The Basic English Skills Test (BEST) is a criterion-referenced, standardized test battery constructed to measure the English language skills of LEP adults. This comprehensive instrument was designed to test communication skills, such as reading, writing, speaking, and listening at a basic functional level. The test kit includes a picture cue book, a test manual, scoring sheets, and student booklets. BEST consists of two subtests.

Basic Inventory of Natural Language. Herbert, C. H. (1983). San Bernardino, CA: Checkpoint Systems, Inc. The Basic Inventory of Natural Language (BINL) is a criterion-referenced test designed to assess the language dominance, proficiency, and growth of students in grades K-12. It focuses on the measurement of oral language, specifically natural speech production in one or more languages. The BINL consists of four kits: forms A and B (grades K-6) and forms C and D (grades 7-12).

Bilingual Syntax Measure II. Burt, M. K., Dulay, H. C., & Hernandez-Chavez, E. (1980). San Antonio, TX: The Psychological Corporation. The Bilingual Syntax Measure II (BSM II) was developed for children in grades K through 3. The focus of the test is on oral syntactical ability derived from students' responses to colorful cartoon representations designed to stimulate the production of specific linguistic structures. The test consists of a 28-cartoon story booklet and a response booklet containing 26 questions.

Comprehensive English Language Test. Harris, D. & Palmer, L. A. (1986). New York: McGraw-Hill Book Co. The Comprehensive English Language Test (CELT) was developed as a test of English language proficiency for high school, college, and adult learners of English as a second or foreign language, particularly at the intermediate and advanced levels. It is a group-administered test with two parallel forms to enhance security and allow for pre- and post-testing. The test is divided into three sections: listening, structure, and vocabulary.

English Language Skills Assessment. Doherty, C., Ilyin, D., Lee, L. F., Levy, L. & Carlton, P. (1980). Scranton, PA: Harper & Row Publishers. The English Language Skills Assessment (ELSA) was designed to assess English as a second language in students from junior high school up to adults. Three levels of difficulty comprise the ELSA: beginner level, consisting of two subtests, a conversation and a narrative; intermediate level, also containing a conversation and a narrative format, and advanced level for which the only subtest is a narrative.

Idea Oral Language Proficiency Test. Ballard, W. S., Tighe, P. L., & Dalton, E. F. (1980). Brea, CA: Ballard and Tighe, Inc. The Idea Oral Language Proficiency Test (IPT 1) was designed to measure the oral proficiency, including comprehension, vocabulary, syntax, morphology, and, at the higher levels, oral creative expression of students in Grades K-6 for whom English is a second or other language. Examinee's individual oral responses to 83 items places them at one of seven proficiency level scores which is used to classify the examinee as non-English, limited English-speaking, or fluent English-speaking (FES).

Interagency Language Roundtable Oral Proficiency Interview. The American Council on the Teaching of Foreign Languages/Educational Testing Service (1982). Princeton, NJ: Educational Testing Service. The Interagency Language Roundtable (TLR) Oral Proficiency Interview (OPT), formerly The Foreign Service Institute Oral Proficiency Interview, was developed by the American Council on the Teaching of Foreign Languages (ACTFL) in cooperation with the Educational Testing Service (ETS) to measure adolescent or adult oral language performance in any language. The focus of the test is on functional performance as well as on the content and accuracy of demonstrated speech.

Language Assessment Battery. New York City Public Schools, Division of Curriculum and Instruction (1982). New York: OREA Scan Center. The Language Assessment Battery (LAB) was developed by the New York City Board of Education to measure the English and Spanish proficiency among Limited English Proficient (LEP) non-native students in grades K-12.

Language Assessment Scales. DeAvila, E. A. & Duncan, S. E. (1981-1982). San Rafael, CA: Linguametrics Group. The Language Assessment Scales (LAS) measures the level of oral language proficiency in English or Spanish. Verbal or motor responses are compared with expected answers or to previously determined standards of production. The test is administered individually, in either English or Spanish, for grades K-5 (Level I), and grades 6-12 and beyond (Level II).

Michigan Test of English Language Proficiency. Upshur, J. (1968-79). Ann Arbor, MI: English Language Institute, University of Michigan. The Michigan Test of English Language Proficiency (MTELP), suitable for group administration, was designed to assess the non-native individual's facility in English at the pre-university and university levels. Widely used as a proficiency test, the MTELP contains sections pertaining to structure, vocabulary, and reading comprehension.

The Oxford Examinations in English as a Foreign Language. Oxford, England: Oxford Delegacy of Local Examinations. The Oxford Examinations in English as a Foreign Language were developed to test performance and receptive skills using nonliterary material in authentic tasks which include writing and reading skills.

Oxford Placement Test. Allan, D. (1982). Oxford, England: Oxford University Press. The Oxford Placement Test (OPT) was designed to measure students' English proficiency and place them into appropriate instructional levels, including elementary to post-proficiency.

The Second Language Oral Test of English. Fathman, A. K. (1983). Hayward, CA: Alemany Press. The Second Language Oral Test of English (SLOTE) was designed to assess the oral language proficiency of non-native speakers of any language background. This

15-minute, criterion-referenced test for grades K-adult is administered individually and scored on the basis of verbal responses to pictures.

Test of English for International Communication (1979). Princeton, NJ: Educational Testing Service. The Test of English for International Communication (TOEIC) is a standardized test used to measure non-native English speakers who will use English in the work force in commerce and industry, in particular in the international trade environment. Its unique aspect is the content which requires that communicative competence in adults be utilized in the seven sub-tests, presented in a multiple choice format.

Test of English Proficiency Level. Rathmell, G. (1985). Hayward, CA: The Alemany Press. The Test of English Proficiency Level (TEPL) was designed to place secondary and adult English as a second language students in one of seven instructional levels in each of four skill areas: (a) oral proficiency, (b) the ability to identify correct structures in sentences, (c) reading comprehension, and (d) the ability to communicate in written English.

Test of Spoken English. Clark, J. L. & Swinton, S. (1980). Princeton, NJ: Educational Testing Service. The Test of Spoken English (TSE) was developed to assess the speaking ability of adults, especially graduate students and professionals whose native language is other than English. Suitable for group administration, this 20-minute exam is administered through the use of a tape recording which elicits oral responses that are recorded and later scored by the Educational Testing Service.

References

Alderson, J. C., Krahnke, K. J. & Stansfield, C. W. (Eds.) (1987). *Reviews of English Language Proficiency.* Washington, DC: Teachers of English to Speakers of Other Languages (TESOL).

Anderson, J. I. (1981). Considerations in phonological assessment. In J. G. Erickson & D. R. Omark (Eds.), *Communication assessment of the bilingual bicultural child: Issues and guidelines* (pp. 77-98). Baltimore, MD: University Park Press.

Bachman, L. F. (1990). Constructing measures and measuring constructs. In B. Harley, P. Allen, J. Cummins & M. Swain (Eds.), *The development of second language proficiency* (pp. 26-38). Cambridge: Cambridge University Press.

Bachman, L. F. & Palmer, A. S. (1982). The construct validation of some components of communicative proficiency. *TESOL Quarterly, 16*(4), 469-465.

Brown, H. (1980). The optimal distance model of second language acquisition. *TESOL Quarterly, 14*, 157-64.

Burt, M. & Dulay, H. (1978). Some guidelines for the assessment of oral language proficiency and dominance. *TESOL Quarterly, 12*(2), 177-192.

Canale, M. & Swain, M. (1980). Theoretical bases of communicative approaches to second language teaching and testing. *Applied Linguistics, 1*(1)1-45.

Canale, M. (1984). A communicative approach to language proficiency assessment in a minority setting. In C. Rivera (Ed.), *Communicative competence approaches to language proficiency assessment: Research and application* (pp. 107-122). Clevedon, Avon: Multilingual Matters Ltd.

Carroll, B. J. (1980). *Testing communicative performance: An interim study.* Oxford: Pergamon Press.

Chomsky, N. (1957). *Syntactic structures.* The Hague: Mouton.

Chomsky, N. (1965). *Aspects of the theory of syntax.* Cambridge, MA: MIT Press.

Cohen, A. (1990). *Language learning.* New York: Newbury House.

Cummins, J. (1979). Linguistic interdependence and the educational development of bilingual children. *Review of Educational Research, 49*(2), 222-251.

Cummins, J. (1980). The cross-lingual dimensions of language proficiency. Implications for bilingual education and the optimal age issue. *TESOL Quarterly, 14,* 157-87.

Cummins, J. (1981). The role of primary language development in promoting educational success for language minority students. In California State Department of Education (Eds.), *Schooling and language minority students (pp. 3-49).* Los Angeles, CA: Evaluation, Dissemination and Assessment Center, California State University.

Cummins, J. (1984). *Bilingualism and special education: Issues in assessment and pedagogy.* San Diego, CA: College-Hill Press.

Cumming, A. (1989). Writing expertise and second-language proficiency. *Language Learning, 39*(1), 81-141.

Day, E. C. (1981). Assessing communicative competence: Integrative testing of second language learners. In J. G. Erickson & D. R. Omark (Eds.), *Communication assessment of the bilingual bicultural child: Issues and guidelines* (pp. 179-197). Baltimore, MD: University Park Press.

Dietrich, T. G., Freeman, C. & Crandall, J. (1979). A linguistic analysis of some English proficiency tests. *TESOL Quarterly, 13*(4), 535-547.

Dulay, H. & Burt, M. (1980). The relative proficiency of limited English proficient students. *NABE Journal, 4*(3), 1-23.

Duran, R. P. (1984). Some implications of communicative competence research for integrative proficiency testing. In C. Rivera (Ed.), *Communicative competence approaches to language proficiency assessment: Research and application* (pp. 44-58). Clevedon, Avon: Multilingual Matters Ltd.

Edelsky, C., Hudelson, S., Flores, B., Barkin, F., Alterweger, B. & Jilbert, K. (1983). Semilingualism and language deficit. *Applied Linguistics, 4*(1), 1-22.

Ellis, R. (1990). *Understanding second language acquisition.* Oxford: Oxford University Press.

Giles, H. & Byrne, J. (1982). An intergroup approach to second language acquisition. *Journal of Multilingual and Multicultural Development, 3*(1), 17-40.

Gleason, J. B. (1989). *The development of language.* Columbus, OH: Merrill.

Harley, B., Allen, P., Cummins, J. & Swain, M. (1990). The nature of language proficiency. In B. Harley, P. Allen, J. Cummins & M. Swain (Eds.), *The development of second language proficiency* (pp. 7-25). Cambridge: Cambridge University Press.

Hakuta, K. (1986). *Mirror of language.* New York: Basic Books.

Hymes, D. (1971). *On communicative competence.* Philadelphia, PA: University of Pennsylvania Press.

Krashen, S. (1981). *Second language acquisition and second language learning.* Oxford: Pergamon.

Krashen, S. (1982). *Principles and practices in second language acquisition.* Oxford: Pergamon.

Labov, W. (1970). *The study of non studied English.* Champaign, IL.: NCTE.

Lambert, W. & Gardner, R. (1972). *Attitudes and motivation in second language learning.* Rowley, MA: Newbury House.

Larsen-Freeman, D. (1991). Second language acquisition research: Staking out the territory. *TESOL Quarterly, 25*(2), 315-350.

Lowe, P. & Stansfield, C. W. (1988). *Second language proficiency assessment.* Englewood Cliffs, NJ: Prentice Hall Regents.

MacNamara, J. (1967). The bilingual's linguistic performance: A psychological overview. *Journal of Social Issues, 23*(2), 58-77.

McCollum, P. (1981). Concepts in bilingualism and their relationship to language assessment. In J. G. Erickson & D. R. Omark (Eds.), *Communication assessment of the bilingual bicultural child: Issues and guidelines* (pp. 25-42). Baltimore, MD: University Park Press.

McLaughlin, B. (1990). The relationship between first and second languages: Language proficiency and language aptitude. In B. Harley, P. Allen, J. Cummins & M. Swain (Eds.), *The development of second language proficiency.* Cambridge: Cambridge University Press.

Oller, J. W. (1979). *Language tests at school: A pragmatic approach.* London: Longman Group.

Oller, J. W. & Perkins, K. (1980) *Research in language testing.* Rowley, MA: Newbury House.

Oller, J. W. (1991). *Language and bilingualism: More tests of tests.* Toronto, Canada; Lewisburg: Bucknell University Press.

Parker, F. (1986). *Linguistics for non-linguists.* Austin, TX: Pro-e.

Phillips, S. (1983). An ethnographic approach to bilingual language proficiency assessment. In C. Rivera (Ed.), *An ethnographic/sociolinguistic approach to language proficiency assessment* (pp. 88-106). Clevedon, Avon: Multilingual Matters Ltd.

Ramirez, A. G. (1984). Pupil characteristics and performance on linguistic and communicative language measures. In C. Rivera (Ed.), *Communicative competence approaches to language proficiency assessment: Research and application* (pp. 82-106). Clevedon, Avon: Multilingual Matters Ltd.

Schumann, J. H. (1986). Research on the acculturation model for second language acquisition. *Journal of multilingual and multicultural development, 7*(5), 379-391.

Snow, C. E. (1992). Perspectives on second-language development: Implications for bilingual education. *Educational Researcher, 21*(2), 16-19.

Spolsky, B. (1989). *Conditions for second language learning.* Oxford: Oxford University Press.

Swain, M. (1985). Communicative competence: Some roles of comprehensible input and comprehensible output in its development. In S. Gass & C. Madden (Eds.), *Input in second language acquisition* (pp. 235-253). Rowley, MA: Newbury House.

Terrell, T. D. (1981). The natural approach in bilingual education. In California State Department of Education (Ed.), *Schooling and language minority students: A theoretical framework* (pp. 117-146). Los Angeles, CA: Evaluation, Dissemination and Assessment Center.

Widdowson, H. G. (1989). Knowledge of language and ability for use. *Applied Linguistics, 10*(2), 128-137.

Zamel, V. (1982). Writing: The process of discovering meaning. *TESOL Quarterly, 16*(2), 195-209.

Zirkel, P. A. (1974). A method for determining and depicting language dominance. *TESOL Quarterly, 8*(1), 7-16.

CHAPTER 5

English as a Second Language Across Grade Levels

The purpose of this chapter is to familiarize the reader with ESL programs in the following school levels: preschool, elementary, secondary and adult programs as they relate to each school's level and educational goals and curricula.

ESL Preschool Programs

Preschool is usually a professional early childhood setting where children play and learn, have a variety of experiences, and meet other children in a friendly atmosphere. Preschool programs can be set in a church, a storefront, or a school building. They can be held in a converted house, a building attached to a factory, or on a college campus. A good preschool setting is always equipped with interesting toys, plenty of books and games, and outdoor space of some kind where a child can run around. It has a professional program, administered by professionally trained, caring adults with whom children can develop close ties and who treat them with respect and affection. The terms nursery schools, preschools, and child care centers are used nearly interchangeably.

Day care and child care centers can be partly or wholly subsidized by government agencies, by private foundations, or by corporations. They can be individually or corporately owned, run for profit or administered as not-for-profit parent cooperatives, and can be part of a chain of centers. Most of the pre-school programs are on a half-day schedule or follow the public school hours. However, because many of

the eligible youngsters come from families in which both parents
work, there is pressure to extend preschool programs to a full day.

A good preschool program takes into consideration the fact that
preschoolers develop at different rates and in different ways. For this
reason, some preschool programs have two-, three-, four-, and five-
year-olds separated, so that they can use the books, toys, and
equipment appropriate to their ages and stages. Some settings simply
have younger or older groups. Still others have older and younger
children separated for certain activities and together for the ones that
are beneficial to both groups.

Language and Reading

Language activities are an important component of most
preschool programs. Book corners, the dictated stories, and charts are
elements of the preschool program that foster literacy, help children
get ready to read and write, and give them a strong sense that reading
and enjoyment go together (Cazden, 1983; Adams, 1990). No one
knows for sure what age is the best one for beginning to teach reading
or even if there is a best age. Denmark teaches young people to read at
age seven; Israel and Great Britain teach reading at five; the United
States, France, and Japan around age six. There's no evidence that
any one of these timetables is better than the others or that children at
one age learn better than at another. Print awareness begins around
two or three, particularly if children have grown up in a rich language
environment. On their own, children begin to spell their own names,
to recognize other letters, and to be aware that words are the things
between the white spaces on a page. At this stage or later some
children catch on to the fact that people look at words from left to
right and from top to bottom (Huck, 1980). This is a very important
part of getting ready to read. Reading is a skill that comes at least
partly out of experiences in the normal course of children's lives
(Wells, 1986). In other words, the "lessons" are all around. Children
want to know what those signs say. They want to be able to read those
books that can tell them something about a picture that has caught
their eye. They want to recognize their own names and those of their
friends.

Many children have neither the small-motor coordination to be
doing pencil-and-paper drills nor the readiness to sit and attend to
activities that essentially belong to first grade. Some youngsters will

be restless or act up if they are forced to concentrate on tasks that have little developmental appropriateness to them. Or a child may get bored, in which case learning to read later on is likely to become distasteful and a grind rather than a joyful discovery at the optimum time. In a preschool or child care center where teachers have their eye on each child's individual development, children have print all around them and they learn about it each day. There are labels, charts, and names everywhere, but no one necessarily makes a lesson of these things. Instead, they are there for the children to use as a way of tuning up their eyes and ears. This informality of presenting English print is very important to LEP children since it may be the first experience many of these children have had with the English language. It is expected that many of these preschool children come from non-English speaking homes. And the preschool environment should be flexible enough for them to feel comfortable and ready to learn from the informal learning experiences provided in a language that is not familiar to them.

Everyday Routines

Preschool programs are characterized by the amount of daily routines. Teachers need to integrate the development of English skills into these daily routines. These daily routines are physical play, toilet training, show and tell, and individual activities.

Physical Play. Exercise is not only physical but mental. Physical play under the direction of a trained ESL preschool teacher has limitless extensions and opportunities for learning geared to the developmental and linguistic needs of the child. For example, in a movement class youngsters are encouraged to use the balance beam, where they have to slow down a bit and use control over their body in order to walk the beam. Quieter children are lured into somersaults on the barrel. In movement class, concepts of space are constantly being explored. Children get to understand the concept and the English label for words such as high, low, and medium in a very organic way. Children get the feel of controlling their bodies in space. This is a very important preparation for a host of later physical activities–dancing, competitive games, and team sports. Children may get tired and frustrated too easily with sports, and if they are forced into competition, they get very rigid and cannot do their best. Therefore, games are emphasized where children do what they can and where everyone can come out a winner in some way; where no one person really loses. Children are expanding the English language throughout the game. Children learn to play together well and to appreciate one another in addition to expanding English vocabulary, concepts, and English language structures.

Toileting. Toilet training may be a temporary casualty of preschool, but in the long run much more is learned about bathroom practices than is lost. Children of both sexes become comfortable with toilet routines through seeing other children and sharing information in a casual way. Teachers help children become self-sufficient in the bathroom without blaming or punishing. Children are toileted several times during a morning, and teachers always keep their eyes open for the youngster who has to go and is waiting too long or the one who has just learned control and needs to be helped. Many children who have been using a potty seat at home may need to learn to use a regular toilet. Boys may learn to urinate standing up by watching other boys. Girls and boys learn bathroom routines such as wiping themselves and washing their hands. This is a good opportunity to familiarize children with toileting words, concepts, and phrases.

Show and Tell. Some preschools call it "sharing time." Others call it "circle time," because often the children sit in a circle for this activity. Show-and-tell is very much part of almost every preschool curriculum and part of many kindergarten programs as well. The main purpose of show-and-tell is for children to share talk, ideas, a special toy or book, or experiences. A teacher usually plans a time or a day and asks the children in the group to bring in an object or tell of an experience that interests them. The children take turns presenting their photo or toy or the leaf that they found on their trip to the country. Other children chime in and ask questions or add to the talk fest. The teacher is there to guide the discussion, but at its best the children often run show-and-tell pretty much on their own. There's a great deal of learning that can come out of these daily exchanges. Children learn to express feelings and ideas and to share them with other children. They get a glimpse into other children's lives and learn about other families and their experiences in a way that is enriching for both the talker and the listener. With LEP children, the teacher carefully has to guide this section to provide a vocabulary and a language structure that to some extent is already part of the children. In this setting, the LEP children can use words from their native language when expressing their ideas. If the teacher is proficient in the home language of the students, the teacher can use this opportunity to provide the words in English and can help them with the structures of the English language in a non-threatening way.

Child to Child. A good preschool program recognizes that children learn from one another. Teachers are well aware of their students' individual needs each day, and many activities are done in groups. Being with other children and interacting with them is a very important aspect of this age, since it offers children the opportunity to interact with both older and younger children in a safe, constructive way. If there are English proficient students in the classroom, this is a good opportunity for LEP children to hear English and begin to use it in interactive ways.

Recommended ESL Instructional Strategies

The pre-school program provides the ideal language curriculum for LEP children to begin listening and increasing English use. The following are instructional recommendations:

1. Limited English proficient children will be more likely to understand what is expected of them when regular preschool routines are followed consistently from the beginning of the year, so that if they do not understand the language at least they can follow the action implied in the routine. One routine, circle time, is particularly important as it provides the children with a feeling of group identity and introduces them to a variety of cultures represented in the class. At first, however, the teacher should limit the size of the circle and the length of time the children are expected to participate as well as simplify the English language used (vocabulary and structures), or they may easily feel overwhelmed.
2. Songs and stories presented in class should be simple and repeated frequently. Visual aids (felt boards, small objects, pictures, photographs) help to reinforce the meaning of new vocabulary and sentences. Opportunities for non-verbal responses need to be given whenever possible, particularly early in the year when the children are not yet able to express themselves in English.
3. The teacher may also find that at the beginning of the year some

children feel more comfortable playing outdoors, if there are organized games such as follow-the-leader. Indoor activities that include nonverbal communication are simple charades, action songs, and stories set to movement, all of which help children to feel involved in the preschool classroom.

4. Objects familiar to the children should be included as much as possible in the classroom setting. Appropriate objects are cooking utensils (such as a wok or bamboo steamer), clothing (such as saris and kimonos), and authentic games and toys from the different cultures represented by the children.

5. Preschool programs usually provide children with about an hour of free-play time during each session, but some children in the ESL classroom require help in developing skills needed to benefit from this period. Dramatic play, for instance, may take longer to evolve because of the initial inability to communicate in a common language (and this may also have restricted the children's previous play experience with peers in the home neighborhood). In early stages the teacher can provide extra support by directly participating in the action, using props and toys to stimulate cooperative play, and showing how the activity can be varied or extended. The children are thus encouraged to continue playing without the teacher.

6. Activities designed to achieve a common goal are always helpful for encouraging cooperation and language usage of children within small groups. Suitable activities include buying and cooking food (such as applesauce), indoor gardening, and care of classroom pets. In addition, planning these experiences gives the teacher the means to overcome the typical problem of children remaining all year with friends from the same cultural and linguistic group.

7. Adequate amounts of paint, crayons, paper, and modeling materials should be available to develop imagination and creativity. If students prefer to paint or draw in their native language, they should be allowed to do it. The most important aspect to consider is their sense of belonging in the group and opportunities to interact in English with the teacher and with English specific peers. Parents will also be more accepting of materials like finger-painting when they can see their children using them with enjoyment and enthusiasm.

ESL in the Elementary School

The function of the elementary school is to help students to: (a) understand and practice desirable social relationships, (b) discover and develop their own desirable individual aptitudes, (c) cultivate the habit of critical thinking, (d) appreciate and desire worthwhile activities, (e) gain command of common integrating knowledge and skills, and (f) develop a positive physical and mental attitude (Klein, 1989; Goodlad, 1984; Purkey & Smith, 1983; Wright, 1980). Elementary schools are readily associated with such subjects as reading, spelling, language arts, quantitative relationships of arithmetic or mathematics, science and social studies, art, music, and physical education. Another function of the elementary school is the development of social relations, ethical behavior, and the social and emotional development of the individual. To achieve knowledge and skills in these objectives, subject area interactions between teacher and students and among the students themselves are a prerequisite. Certain of the above objectives are achieved better than others. Objectives such as economic efficiency or civic responsibility are emphasized more in the secondary than in the elementary school but are not excluded from the elementary school curriculum.

Providing students with opportunities to meet the above objectives will prepare them to meet the challenges of a rapidly changing world. Students will meet these challenges if they can demonstrate competence in critical thinking, reasoning skills, synthesis of knowledge, humanistic understanding, social awareness, creativity, and self-esteem. More specifically, the elementary school provides a specific curriculum in which students are provided with a variety of rich opportunities to: (a) think logically and creatively; (b) apply reasoning skills to issues and problems; (c) comprehend written, spoken, and visual presentations in various medias; (d) speak, listen to, read and write clearly and effectively in English; (e) perform basic mathematical calculations; (f) speak, listen to, read and write at least one language other than English; (g) use current and developing technologies for academic and occupational pursuits, and (h) determine what information is needed for particular purposes and be able to acquire, organize, and use that information for those purposes.

The "effective schools" research (Purkey & Smith, 1983) identified certain characteristics of the nature of elementary schools that are especially facilitative in meeting those objectives as they relate to high achievement test scores: (a) high expectations for recognition of academic achievement, (b) a safe and orderly environment, (c) collegial relationship among staff members, (e) a sense of community, and (f) parental involvement and support. Elementary schools provide all students with a curriculum that help all of them achieve these goals. Limited English proficient children, due to their limitation with the English language, need specific instructional strategies to accomplish the above goals and objectives. The goals of second language teaching (in the case of English) are the achievement of functional communication in the context of the target language as well as providing students with the cognitive/academic skills outlined before. English as a second language programs at the elementary level need to help students meet the above objectives.

ESL Strategies

There is a tremendous number of strategies that can be incorporated into the elementary classroom. All the approaches mentioned in Chapter 7 are part of the methodologies used in successful ESL elementary school classrooms. The list that follows provides specific recommended activities to help teachers provide a curriculum to LEP children that is understandable, meaningful, and at the same time helps them meet the goals of the elementary school mentioned in the previous section. Some examples are:

1. Using students and the teacher themselves (their clothing, the things they carry) to teach appropriate vocabulary before using pictures or other materials.
2. Using the known environment of the students before fanning out to the wider English-speaking world, relating the presentations to facets of language or of culture which the teacher can expect the students to be familiar with.
3. Using dialogues wherever possible, since dialogues duplicate the communication situations in everyday life. It is a good idea to keep building on the same dialogue situation where possible.
4. Planning as many different oral practice activities for each lesson as possible.

5. Using the students' native language judiciously when it will mean saving time or insuring comprehension.
6. Encouraging students to prepare materials. Teachers should ask students to find pictures, to cut and mount them, to prepare flashcards, to draw pictures, and even to compose or build a dialogue with new words or structures they have learned. Students should be encouraged to write short conversations or plays which can later be dramatized.
7. Simplifying and adapting stories which the teacher can tell the students. If there are duplicating facilities, preparing simplified material for reading is recommended.
8. Creating a "cultural island" in the room. It can be done by having pictures, maps, bulletin boards, proverbs, and labels in English.
9. Utilizing the community resources and bringing the people in the community into the program. This is important not only because it provides additional stimulation for the students but also because it will foster interest in English language learning in the community.
   - Asking English speakers to come to the classroom to speak about their trips, hobbies, interests, or jobs. The preparation for the visit should include listening to the speech and writing a letter of thanks to the visitor, leading naturally to language learning.
   - Starting an English club to which community members may be invited, and planning topics for discussion or games and songs around the interests of the students.
   - Asking the local resources (if possible) to help students print an English (or bilingual) newspaper.
   - Preparing simple plays to which parents and other lay people in the community are invited.
10. Utilizing the incidental happenings in the school or the immediate community to teach or to review language items. The use of special events and incidental happenings not only extends knowledge but also illustrates that the structures or vocabulary practiced within one situation can be used to talk about another.
11. Giving students the feeling and the assurance that English is a vehicle of communication which serves exactly the same

purposes as does the students' native tongue. What do people all over the world generally talk about? The daily routine of sleeping, eating, shopping, working, and playing; age; births; marriage and illness are good examples. Although it is true that people use different words and expressions, there are equivalent expressions to discuss equivalent events in any culture.

12. Providing opportunities for students to act as listeners and as speakers. Students should be able not only to make statements but also to make comments or responses, to ask questions, and to answer questions.

13. Using authentic language at normal speed in the classroom. Often, in the desire to simplify language for LEP students, teachers give expressions or words which they consider easier simply because they are shorter. But teachers need to remember that sometimes the longer word may be more similar to a cognate in the students' language. Also, since everything is different for learners, they may just as well learn the expressions or words that native speakers of their age would generally employ in similar circumstances.

ESL in the Secondary School

Secondary schools' main goal is the continuation of educational experiences for students in their development of thinking skills through involvement in intellectual, civic/social, personal, and career curricula (Boyer, 1983; Resnick & Klopfer, 1989). Much literature on secondary schools mentions the issue of school reform (Boyer, 1983; Posner, 1990) for guiding schools in achieving higher standards, more time on tasks, stronger academic courses, an extended school day and year, more homework, and revised teacher preparation. The goals of the secondary schools have been grouped in five general areas: intellectual; civic, social; personal, moral, aesthetic; economic, vocational; and individual. Components in each of these areas are listed below.

Intellectual: (a) *gain* a "fund of information"; (b) *learn* efficient use of reading, writing, and computational skills to acquire and communicate knowledge; (c) *acquire* the habit of weighing facts and imaginatively apply them; and (d) *acquire* a continuing desire for knowledge.

Civic/social: (a) *learn* compassion for others and *learn* to live and work in harmony, (b) *gain* an understanding of government and a sense of civic responsibility, (c) *learn* loyalty to the United States, and (d) *acquire* knowledge of world affairs.

Personal/moral/aesthetic: (a) *develop* a well-cared-for own body, (b) *develop* a sense of right and wrong, and (c) *learn* to enjoy cultural activities.

Economic/vocational: (a) *receive* information and guidance in making occupational choices, (b) *receive* specialized training in a specific job, (c) *learn* homemaking and handy-man skills, and (d) *learn* to manage personal finances.

The above goals provide the theoretical framework for educators to provide students with educational activities as a means of meeting their cognitive, academic, and social needs. These are meant to help students participate in active learning, cooperative work, and to have individual responsibility toward the core curriculum of mathematics, science, English, social studies, foreign languages or among other subjects prescribed by the school curriculum. For example, in the area of communication arts which are the concern of this book general goals of the secondary school include to:

1. *Appreciating* the role that language plays in understanding all subjects, in achieving success in life, and in communicating with all people.
2. *Learning* to communicate effectively through the integration of their studies to develop skills in grammar, composition, literature, vocabulary, library use, oral communication, and interpretation.
3. *Gaining* information, discovering meanings, understanding logical relationships, and making judgments through critical listening and reading.
4. *Speaking,* writing, and solving problems creatively and confidently with a sense of audience.
5. *Communicating* emotions, ideas, opinions, values, and experiences.
6. *Reading* to discover the power and beauty of literature as a mirror of human experience.

7. *Applying* analysis, synthesis, and evaluation/criticism skills in thinking and writing.

In general, ESL programs in the secondary school group students by levels. The three traditional levels of beginning, intermediate, and advanced are still the organization of many ESL programs. These levels provide students with challenges, access to the curriculum, and opportunities that are available to all students, although the process and approaches to arrive at these goals differ. The goal of ESL programs is to assist LEP students in achieving fluency (including listening comprehension, speaking, reading, and writing skills) in English.

At the beginning level, the ESL program goals are to help LEP students to be able to discriminate and produce sounds of English and basic intonation patterns, comprehend routine classroom directions, draw inferences and conclusions based on oral communication, produce sentences, acquire competence in beginning grammatical structures, understand and use beginning-level vocabulary, comprehend short passages, write guided compositions, use basic punctuation marks, and acquire a knowledge of their new cultural environment. At the intermediate level students are challenged to refine production of the sounds of English, improve their ability to understand and produce fluent speech, acquire functional competence in use of intermediate-level grammatical structures, expand vocabulary through acquisition of vocabulary and idiomatic expression, read short selections of prose and poetry, identify sequence of events; recognize cause and effect, perceive organization and use of contextual clues, read for enjoyment, read in the content areas, write short paragraphs, personal letters, and book reports; write free compositions; and augment their knowledge and understanding of the new culture. At the advanced and transitional levels, students are directed to comprehend and produce complex connected discourses; answer all manner of questions with communicative and linguistic competence; comprehend passages with interpretive expression; participate successfully in all class discussions; give oral presentations; acquire functional competence in grammatical structures at this level; expand vocabulary, comprehend content area materials; read selections of increased difficulty; demonstrate skill in interpretive and critical reading; be able to scan; use reference materials; be familiar with works of well-known writers; write coherent compositions; and increase their knowledge of the culture of the people of the United States.

ESL should be a function of the total curriculum with the teaching of vocabulary and concepts of the content areas. It is accomplished through an ESL approach, in which content and language teaching are integrated. Language is everybody's business and everybody's responsibility. Content-area teachers adapt their curriculum and their teaching styles to include students who are less than proficient in English; ESL teachers use subject area content to teach the structure and function of the English language. Figure 5.1 presents a summary of characteristics that may be shared by students at the secondary level.

Figure 5.1. Characteristics of LEP Students at the Secondary Level.

Academic Skills

a. Less oral participation in class.
b. Discrepancy between oral and written skills.
c. Inexperience in group work.
d. Dependence on following teacher's instructions rather than using own initiative.
e. Discrepancy between subject area skills in mathematics, social studies, and English language skills.
f. Possessing talents that may not show up in class (artistic, musical, leadership, etc.).

Classroom Behavior

a. Fear of being the leader.
b. Feeling isolated in the class.
c. Inclination to share and help other students (seen in our culture as cheating).
d. Taking everything a teacher says seriously.
e. Fear of asking for help even after progress reports and other warnings.
f. Respect for authoritarian figures.

Home/Cultural Influences

a. Traditional ideas about roles of males and females.
b. High expectations for boys to succeed.
c. Not living in a nuclear family.

Language Behaviors	
a. Memorize functional expressions.	h. Retain information.
b. May not appear to retain vocabulary or structure.	i. Has developed several effective strategies for language learning.
c. Share a sense of helplessness.	j. Use synonyms; uses language to learn.
d. Use limited structures and vocabulary.	
e. Use language very literally.	k. Has ability to initiate conversation.
f. Concrete experiences important.	l. Rely more on print and on listening.
g. Relabel concepts from first language.	

Instructional Strategies

Research has shown that reading, writing, speaking, and listening are all parts of students' general development and should not be see; as discrete skills to be taught in isolation. Learning is not separate from meaning and divided into separate activities such as penmanship, phonics, or spelling (Bell & Burnalby, 1984).   The focus is on "meaning-making."   What this means for the teacher is that opportunities for reading, writing, speaking, and listening must be presented; that situations must be meaningful; and that the learning situations must also be integrated so that all four skills are used together.

Students in secondary schools read a great deal in all subject areas. Reading is made up of many components, but focusing on each skill in isolation is counterproductive. The program and the teacher must create a balance between making materials available and consciously directing the students' acquisition of reading skills. Thus, LEP students need to be immersed in real reading. They also need a wealth of materials that they are capable of reading, a helpful guide, and an enabling environment.

Writing is an important skill at the secondary school level. Writing is a cyclical process, in which the writer continually circles back, reviewing and revising. Writers learn to write by writing. For LEP students, time must be provided to work through the stages of the writing process: thinking about a topic, organizing, drafting, evaluating, revising, and editing. To write well every beginning writer needs to be immersed in writing, an enabling environment, and feedback and guidance from interested readers. To immerse students in writing a teacher needs to make writing an everyday activity. Prerequisites include: (a) make writing real, (b) make writing meaningful, (c) allow students to explore all forms of writing (poetry, essays), and (d) provide time for both intensive (structured) and extensive (creative) writing. An enabling environment creates a comfortable atmosphere (makes writing a collaborative act, celebrates students' writing, and allows students to write in their own language to model the writing process if necessary).

Emphasis needs to be put on developing competency in listening and speaking. To develop this competency LEP students need: (a) teachers who understand the stages of second language acquisition and adjust input to fit each student's level; (b) teachers who are tolerant of errors, enabling students to learn without being punished for their pronunciation or word-choice errors; and (c) many opportunities to talk, listen, and interact with others.

In teaching pre-literate non-English-speaking students, teachers will want to focus on oral language development in both the first language and English at different times of the day. Activities may include listening to and watching films; giving story dictations to the teacher that will then be read back; reading in the first language through "language experience"; and group story writing and reading back in either first language or in English. If students are literate in their own language and are at (or close to) grade level in content, teachers can proceed with grade level curriculum using an ESL instructional methodology.

ESL Programs for Adults

The field of adult ESL has changed tremendously over the past twenty years. Curricula, teaching methods and techniques, instructional materials, and assessment instruments have been developed to bring both the student and the classroom closer to the language needs of the adult population. There are several types of adult ESL programs. The most popular ones are: (a) ESL Survival/Basic Skills, (b) ESL in the Workplace, (c) ESL for Specific

Purposes, and (d) College Level ESL. Adult teaching situations and the types of students vary from place to place. These programs are briefly discussed below.

ESL Survival/Basic Skills

In recent years large numbers of adult refugees and immigrants with varied experiences in classroom learning situations have enrolled in ESL programs. These adults have an immediate need for English language survival skills as well as the minimum language skills necessary to obtain an entry-level job. They need language instruction that is both effective and time efficient. Adult refugees and immigrants simply do not have the luxury of spending twenty, ten, or even five hours a week for one or two years in a traditional ESL program to learn the language; nor, in fact, is there any assurance that a great deal of time spent in such a program would provide these learners with what they actually need. Adult learners have work obligations and family and community responsibilities that must be fulfilled; therefore, they are entitled to language training that is relevant, flexible, effective, and efficient. Figure 5.2 illustrates goals of most ESL survival programs, which take into consideration learners' needs and interests.

Adult ESL classes are generally organized as part of a community adult school program, funded by local school district taxes, and housed in local high schools or college buildings. Usually, courses are available to anyone currently residing in the community. A record is kept of the students' attendance, so that individuals can get credit where appropriate, but registration is allowed continuously throughout a semester allowing students to enter a class at any time. The students in an adult class are usually working people reflecting different occupations, from waiters to mechanics, to nurses and medical assistants. It is not easy to make simple classifications of people attending adult ESL classes. The range of interests and learning goals of the students will be as widely varied as their occupations. Also, the constitution of a class tends to be very fluid from one level to the next.

Figure 5.2 Survival ESL: General Knowledge and Content Areas

BASIC SKILLS	CONSUMER ECONOMICS	OCCUPATION/ KNOWLEDGE	HEALTH	COMMUNITY RESOURCES	GOVERNMENT AND LAW
Reading	Read a sales ad	Read a job description	Read first aid directions	Read a movie schedule	Read about rights after being arrested
Writing	Share an ethnic recipe	Fill out a job application	Complete a medical history form	Write a letter to the school	Write a complaint letter
Speaking Listening	Ask questions about buying	Follow job safety rules	Follow a doctor's advice	Use the telephone	Describe an accident
Problem Solving	Describe which apartment is best	Decide which job is better	Decide which hospital to go to in an emergency	Be able to use machines in the bank	Decide which candidate to vote for
Interpersonal Relations	Relate to a sales clerk successfully	Succeed in a job interview	Speak to a doctor	Ask directions	Interact with police
Compu-tation	Compute sales tax	Calculate paycheck deductions	Understand hospital bills	Calculate how much to spend in the supermarket	Explain tax deductions

Because of job moves, family obligations, military reassignments or simply a return to their home country, many students drop out of sequence at the end of the semester or at midway into the course. Another impediment of progress in ESL is the lack of literacy development in the students' native language. Many of them have been self-supporting for a large proportion of their lives and did not have the opportunity to attend secondary schools in their home countries. For this reason, during the past years great attention has been given to adult ESL literacy programs (Bell and Burnalby, 1984). Thus, the variety of school background as well as learning rates demand an individualized ESL approach (Chall, Heron & Hilferty, 1987).

In survival ESL programs the following aspects are important to consider:

Relevancy. Adults are likely to learn more easily when the usefulness in regard to common tasks is clear.

Motivation. In order to keep motivation high, language cannot be taught in isolation. For example, teaching the present perfect tense for its own sake is rarely a motivating force. When the present perfect tense is necessary to perform a certain competency, then it is learned since it becomes relevant to students.

Concrete goals. Students know what is expected of them, thus decreasing the natural feeling of anxiety when facing the unknown.

Flexibility. Students are not expected to learn the entire language (all the verb tenses, for example) before using it. Adult students have immediate needs, and the language needed for a specific competency can be taught and used immediately. Furthermore, ESL is flexible in terms of the various means available for achieving its goals. Teachers can use their preferred methods, materials, and techniques or any combination of methods. This also gives the student more variety, which is desirable since some students learn better by one method than another.

Opportunity for individualization. Students can develop competencies at their own pace; some will master the competencies faster than others. Since many of the language skills required to perform a certain competency will be reintroduced in the learning of other competencies, the content of the lessons is naturally recycled. Moreover, students can develop competencies at their own level of language ability.

ESL in the Workplace

Over the past decade English language programs have become increasingly specialized. One of these areas of specialization is the teaching of linguistic skills in the context of a job. What is new about this approach is that it looks at the learner and the purposes for which the target language is required. It is on this assessment of purposes and needs that the entire program of ESL in the workplace is built. This specialized approach is part of a larger movement within the language-teaching profession away from a concentration on structures to an emphasis on language in context or use. In emphasizing functional language, a variety of programs have been developed that move the English language program away from the classroom and into the work site. These vocational English as a second language courses may be offered as individual programs, on an as-needed basis, or as part of a larger vocational training program. It is possible to develop an integrated program that teaches job skills and the language skills one needs to function on that particular job.

English for Specific Purposes

English for specific purposes is international in scope and specific in purpose (Swales, 1988). Students come from different countries and different backgrounds. However, all of them have a unique purpose, to learn sufficient English for chosen communicative environments: the field of medicine, the field of engineering, the field of commerce, and many others. The English for specific purposes (ESP) program comes from the assumption that learners need to see the necessity in learning the language. The major professional/career field of the ESL students is targeted, such as English for engineers, chemists, nurses, and the like. Language is for a number of specific purposes, each with a variety of possible contents. Students are motivated to feel that their language needs are fulfilled through a solid, flexible basic course, in which the student can later develop diversifications of language use for specific purposes. The curriculum focuses on the students' various needs: skills, topics, and functions. Students are introduced to the various benefits of language study, interpersonal, cultural, expressive, global and professional. English for specific purposes prepares students for a certain task or occupation with a definable goal. It focuses on the communicative as well as the written needs of professionals and workers, giving primary importance to many foreign language professional environments.

College Level ESL

College ESL students are usually immigrants and foreign students. They come to the ESL classroom with the aspirations of completing an academic program in an English-speaking academic environment. They need English survival skills to manage English classrooms and library work. Some adult students are in the United States on special visa programs which allow them to take a specific course of study at a specific school. They are required to take a full-time schedule. They often make up a considerable proportion of daytime ESL classes. In general, these college ESL students have a high degree of literacy development within their native language.

Another group of ESL students are resident students, who, according to college English proficiency measures, are considered non-native speakers, who want to follow a regular course of study leading mainly to an associate or bachelor's degree. The sequence of the ESL program provides educational experiences in speaking, listening, reading, and writing English until students enter a full program of study conducted in English. Usually, the ESL program is divided in levels (usually three to five levels) based on English proficiency assessment scores. Eventual exit from the program is determined by the students' score in written and oral proficiency tests.

References

Adams, M. J. (1990). *Beginning to read. Thinking and learning about print.* Cambridge, MA: The MIT Press.

Bailey, N. C., Madden, C. & Krashen, S. (1983). Is there a "natural sequence" in adult second language learning? *Language Learning, 24,* 235-244

Bell, J. & Burnalby, B. (1984). *A handbook for ESL literacy.* Toronto: OISE Press.

Boyer, E. L. (1983). *High school: A report of the Carnegie Foundation for the advancement of teaching.* New York: Harper & Row.

Cazden, C. (1983). Adult assistance to language development. Scaffolds, models and direct instruction. In R. N. Parker & T. A. Davis (Eds.), *Developing literacy: Young children's use of language* (pp. 3-18). Newark: International Reading Associates.

Chall, J., Heron, E. & Hilferty, A. (1987). Adult literacy: New and enduring problems. *Phi Delta Kappan, 69,* 190-196.

Goodlad, J. I. (1984). *A place called school: Prospects for the future.* New York: McGraw-Hill.

Huck, C. (1980). Teacher feature. The W.E.B. *Learning to read naturally, 4*(4), 14-17.

Klein, M. F. (1989). *Curriculum reform in the elementary school: Creating your own agenda.* New York: Teachers College Press.

Posner, G. J. (1990). *Analyzing the curriculum.* New York: McGraw-Hill.

Purkey, S. C. & Smith, M. S. (1983). Effective schools: A review. *The Elementary School Journal, 83*(4), 427-452.

Resnik, L. B. & Klopfer, L. E. (1989). Toward the thinking curriculum: An overview. In L. B. Resnick & L. E. Klopfer (Eds.), *Toward the thinking curriculum: Current cognitive research* (pp. 1-18), Washington, DC: ASCII.

Swales, J. M. (1988). *Episodes of ESP: A source and reference book for the development of English for science and technology.* New York: Prentice Hall.

Wells, G. (1986). *The meaning makers: Children learning language and using language to learn.* Portsmouth, NH: Heinemann.

Wright, J. E. (1980). *Teaching and learning. A study of schooling.* (Report No. 18, ERIC Document Reproduction Service No. ED214888).

CHAPTER 6

English As a Second Language Programs

The literature on ESL programs is confusing when it comes to naming and defining the variations in ESL program designs which have been implemented, especially in the United States over the last 30 years. Although the main objective of an ESL program is the teaching and learning of English, there are different types of ESL programs. Differences in programs depend on the educational goals of the school and the community, availability of ESL personnel, and the amount of non-English speakers or limited English proficient students in a given school or grade as well as the perception of school instructional leaders of the organization, scope, and sequence needed to learn English. This last aspect has not been quite understood by school personnel in charge of providing students with a complete ESL program, who many times have opted for providing LEP students with minimum ESL instructional services. This chapter describes existing ESL programs as well as identifying optimal and desirable objectives of each of them to meet the linguistic, cognitive, and academic needs of LEP students.

Free Standing ESL Programs

Many of the students enrolled in ESL classes are in these classes because they do not have the necessary English skills to function in an all-English curriculum. Free standing ESL is a recommended program when there are many languages or ethnic groups represented in the school and not too many students from one particular language, making English the only feasible approach for instruction. Another reason for choosing this approach is because the school or the community considers this approach, regardless of the number of LEP students or languages involved, to be the one best suited to local desires and educational objectives. This model provides ESL students with one hour to a whole day of instruction in an ESL format. Free standing is a term commonly used in New York State to differentiate an ESL program that stands by itself, in which English is the only medium of instruction. It is a teaching approach designed to meet the immediate communication and academic needs of the students whose proficiency in English is limited or non-existent. The program provides students with the language skills they need to communicate with teachers and peers and to receive content matter in English (New York State Education Department, 1988). In this model their instruction is based on a special curriculum that typically involves very little or no use of the native language and is usually taught in specific periods. There are variations of free standing ESL programs; wholistic, intensive, and pull-out are the most known.

Wholistic ESL Programs

This is one of the most recommended ESL program designs. This model provides LEP students with instruction totally in an ESL format, introducing content area subjects as well as language skills at students' level of English language proficiency. This design uses the curriculum of the content areas providing teachers with more alternatives to present the English language, less focus on language itself, and more emphasis on hands-on, motivating tasks in content such as mathematics, science, and social studies which encourage natural acquisition. As LEP students increase their mastery of English, they are gradually moved into academic classes with native speakers of English or continue with other limited proficient English speakers at their own level. This program requires school districts to have a large population of LEP students, content area teachers trained in ESL methodologies, as well as curriculum specialists who can help teachers design the program. La Guardia International High School in New York City is a public school which follows this program design.

Intensive ESL Programs

This program consists of all day or half day intensive ESL classes in which English is reinforced in all the subject areas. The main purpose of this program is to provide students with a short and intensive English program including survival skills in the four areas, as well as immediate academic language to be able to function as quickly as possible in the mainstream English-only classroom. When non-English speakers, especially high school students or adults, arrive in the United States and are enrolled in school, some school districts may initially provide an intensive ESL program to help them become familiar with the English language and the school environment.

Pull-out Programs

ESL instruction is composed of English taught from a second language point of view in language arts classes provided at the students' level of English proficiency. In ESL pull-out programs students usually receive forty-five minutes to one hour of instruction in segregated ESL centers or classes. Usually ESL teachers have a small room shared with other programs. The teacher usually goes classroom by classroom to get the ESL students and gather them in the ESL classroom. Because students are from different grade levels and programs, the ESL teacher has difficulties in adapting the ESL instruction to students' content areas. When there are just a few LEP students in each school or district, itinerant ESL teachers may have to travel to several schools in one day or week to meet the English language needs of students. Because of all of the above limitations this ESL program is perceived by school personnel, parents, and students as compensatory or remedial classes for students with learning and language problems.

ESL in Bilingual Education

Bilingual instruction is the preferred model for instructing LEP students (TESOL, 1976). Bilingual education is an educational process which focuses on the students' total development, and capitalizes on students' proficiency in the primary language and their familiarity with their own culture while simultaneously developing the students' competencies in English. The instructional use and development of the students' non-English native language promote students' self-esteem, subject matter achievement, and English language acquisition. English as a second language is an essential and integral part of bilingual education. The ESL component of the bilingual education program recognizes that students may have developed proficiency in one or all of the areas of language in their primary language. The ESL component capitalizes on this proficiency in order to accelerate the process of acquiring the English language. There are a variety of bilingual education programs. These are briefly described below.

Transitional Bilingual Education

This is a program of instruction designed for children of limited English proficiency in elementary, secondary schools, or college settings which provides structured English language instruction and native language instruction (Public Law 100-297, 1988). Native language instruction is provided to avoid loss of grade-level skills while mastery of a second language is taking place. Classes in content areas (i.e., mathematics, science, social studies) are taught in the first language to help students master course content without losing time while second language proficiency is being developed. The instruction incorporates cultural heritage of the students served and the culture of other students in American society (Public Law 100-297, 1988). Transitional classes can keep students at grade level while learning a second language and can aid those below grade level to catch up with their peers through intensive instruction in a language the student fully understands (Carrasquillo, 1991; Crawford, 1989). The main objective of this program is for the students to achieve competence in the English language. As soon as students are considered proficient enough in English to work academically in all-English classes, they are transferred from the bilingual program into monolingual classes with English speaking students. Most transitional programs exit students into an all-English classroom after a maximum of two to three years in bilingual classes.

Developmental Bilingual Education

This is a program, usually at the elementary, secondary, or college level, which provides structured English language instruction in the students' native language (Public Law 100-297, 1988). In the United States developmental bilingual programs' main objective is that students receive a solid academic curriculum with support for reaching full-English language proficiency without negating students' first language development. The objective of this program is to help children achieve competence in English and the native language while mastering subject matter skills. The instruction, to the extent necessary and possible, in all courses or subjects of study is provided in both languages which will allow students to meet grade-promotion and graduation standards. Developmental programs would include classes taught in both languages in a multicultural curriculum. Developmental programs have become an issue of great importance for communities that wish to maintain their ethnic heritage. Another name found in the literature for this program is maintenance bilingual education, since in the United States the native language of the students is maintained or used in the curriculum.

Two-Way Bilingual Program

Two-way bilingual education refers to an integrated model in which speakers of two languages are placed together in a bilingual classroom to learn each other's language and work academically in both languages (Snow, 1986). For example, English-only students learn Spanish as a second language while continuing to develop their native English language skills and LEP students learn English as a second language while becoming literate in their native language (Snow, 1986). Two-way is an effective approach of teaching a second language to English-dominant students in the United States as well as providing an integrated class for language minority students. Baecher (1991) cites authorities which have identified unique features of two-way bilingual programs. These are:

1. They bring together two distinct target groups–the language minority as well as the language majority student–who learns in the same classroom.
2. The native language of each group is carefully developed through appropriate language arts and academic subject material, while second language learning is fostered.
3. The goals are functional bilinguals in both languages and greater intercultural understanding. (p. 83)

Bilingual programs–transitional, maintenance, two-way bilingual programs–recognize the need to teach: (a) the students' primary language, (b) the content matter (subject areas) through the primary language, (c) the history and cultural heritage of both linguistic groups, and (d) English as a second language. ESL instruction in a bilingual classroom includes English taught using ESL methodologies in the language arts and reading and content area instruction in English provided at the students' level of English proficiency. Most two-way bilingual programs keep students in the program as long as possible since bilingualism is a goal of these programs.

Special Alternative Instructional Programs

The federal government in the 1988 Public Law defines these as those that have specially designed curricula and are appropriate for the particular English needs of the children enrolled (Public Law 100-297). These programs provide structured English language instruction and special instructional services which allow students to achieve competence in English language to meet grade-promotion and graduation standards. These programs usually combine a series of ESL methodologies such as sheltered English, English in the content areas, literature based, with the main purpose of providing students with an enriched language program to meet the English language deficits of LEP students.

Immersion Programs

Immersion programs are less practiced in the United States but used extensively in Canada. In the United States, there have been two types of immersion programs. One is directed toward mainstream English-speaking students and has bilingualism as a goal. The other type is directed toward LEP students and has English monolingualism as its goal. For LEP students the goal of this program is to give students the general language skills and the specific academic literacy skills they need to compete with native English-speaking children. Students are taught in a second language from the first year of school with first-language instruction mostly for guidance purposes. Usually, teachers in such programs are bilingual and accept students' responses in first language but respond only in English. According to Krashen (1981, 1982) the success of immersion programs is due to the fact that comprehensible input, which he sees as the only true cause of second language acquisition, has been provided through subject matter teaching. However, Allen, Swain, Harley and Cummins (1990) suggest that not all content teaching is necessarily good language teaching, since typical content teaching focuses on meaning comprehension, and second language learners need to focus on forming meaning relationships.

Another term used in the literature is structured immersion. Structured immersion focuses on providing LEP students English language instruction using content area English. Since the main goal of the program is improved academic performance in English, the materials used are highly structured to introduce academic content using second language methodologies.

References

Allen, P., Swain, M., Harley, B. & Cummins, J. (1990). Aspects of classroom treatment: Toward a more comprehensive view of second language education. In Harley, B., Allen, P., Cummins, J. and Swain, M. (Eds.), *The development of second language proficiency* (pp. 57-81). New York: Cambridge University Press.

Baecher, R. E. (1991). Language learning for success: The promise and practice of two-way bilingual programs. In A. Carrasquillo (Ed.), *Bilingual education: Using languages for success* (pp. 81-95). New York: New York State Association for Bilingual Education.

Carrasquillo, A. (1991). *Bilingual education: Using languages for success.* New York: New York State Association for Bilingual Education.

Crawford, J. (1989). *Bilingual education: History, politics, theory, and practice.* Trenton, NJ: Crane.

Krashen, S. D. (1981). *Second language acquisition and second language learning.* Oxford: Pergamon Press.

Krashen, S. D. (1982). *Principles and practices in second language acquisition.* Oxford: Pergamon Press.

New York State Education Department (1988). *Regents policy paper and proposed action plan for bilingual education.* New York: New York State Education Report.

Snow, M. (1986). *Common terms in second language education.* Education Report Series, No. 1. Center for Language Education and Research. Los Angeles, CA: University of California Press.

Teachers of English to Speakers of Other Languages (1976). *Position Paper on the role of English as a second language in bilingual education.* Washington, DC: TESOL.

United States, Public Law 100-297. April 28, 1988. *Bilingual Education Act. Title VII Bilingual Educational Programs.* Washington, DC: Government Printing Office.

CHAPTER 7

Approaches to Second Language Instruction

The ninetics have provided ESL educators with a strong philosophical and empirical background on which to base appropriate instructional practices. The question no longer is what is the best methodology to teach structures, functions, and notions of the English language. The question today is whether or not second language educators are teaching content tasks and processes using English as the medium of instruction and focusing on cooperative, communicative, and student-centered teaching. In developing and carrying out a lesson, educators need to constantly ask themselves: Are my students curious? Do they seem engaged in the content of my lesson? Are the students stimulated by the content and form of the presentation of that content? ESL educators prepare lessons and materials based on the function (meaning/content) and the form (the structure/way of carrying out the meaning) of the language.

The literature describing ESL teaching is abundant in recommending instructional approaches to teaching English to limited English speakers. The knowing "how to do it" is to provide teachers with the opportunity of using strategies that have been used effectively by other ESL educators. These approaches are integrated with subject content in the ESL classroom to maintain the interest and intensity of ESL students on the content of the lesson, and keep them motivated throughout the whole lesson. ESL teachers need to know about these approaches. For a complete historical description of ESL approaches see Richards and Rodgers (1986). This chapter describes only those instructional approaches considered by the author to be successful (to attend to form and meaning) in teaching English. The reader should be aware that some of these approaches are not really a method of teaching, but a philosophy of teaching (i.e., whole language, natural approach).

Whole Language Approach

Whole language is a philosophy of teaching that encourages students to listen, speak, read, and write by building upon the language and experiences of the child (Weaver, 1988). Language learning is integrated in terms of reading, writing, and discussion across subject areas. Language is a functional tool to accomplish real purposes. Weaver (1988) identifies the assumptions of this language approach as follows:

1. Children are expected to learn to read and write as they learned to talk, gradually, naturally, with a minimum of direct instruction, and with encouragement rather than the discouragement of constant corrections.

2. Learning is emphasized more than teaching: the teacher makes detailed observations of the children's needs, then guides their development accordingly.

3. Children read and write every day–and they are never asked to read artificially simplified or contrived language, or to write something that does not have a "real" purpose and audience.

4. Reading, writing, and oral language are not considered separate components of the curriculum, or merely ends in themselves; rather, they permeate everything the children are doing in science, social studies, and the so-called creative arts–drawing, painting, music, and drama.

5. There is no division between first "learning to read" and later "reading to learn," as there is in the code-emphasis, sight words, and basal reading approaches. From the very beginning, children are presented with and encouraged to compose *whole* texts–real language written for real purposes and a real audience. (pp. 44-45)

Whole language programs are commonly found in non-traditional classrooms. Teachers become facilitators in helping students with the topics for writing and the books for reading. Teachers monitor students' activities and hold conferences and small-group instruction when needed. Teachers prepare a rich literary environment which promotes language and learning. Rigg (1991), writing about whole language in ESL contexts, cited several authorities indicating that whole language principles can be applied to ESL classrooms. She indicated that second language classes should offer a language-nurturing environment, paying attention to doing things with language, and second language, like first language, develops through interaction with peers rather than through imitation of teacher's model or through formal study. The holistic ESL class develops a strong sense of community among students and uses a variety of collaborative learning activities. Whole language teachers integrate content area subjects into thematic units; students read for pleasure daily, selecting from a wide variety of materials; students write frequently, sometimes before they read; and there are opportunities to share reading/literature experiences. Weaver's (1988) book is an excellent source of whole language instructional activities.

Natural Approach

The Natural Approach is based on a humanistic theory along with a hypothesis about second language acquisition. This approach focuses on providing a context in the classroom for natural language acquisition to occur, with acquirers receiving maximum "comprehensible input" and establishing the optimal conditions for lowering second language learners' "socio-affective filters" (Krashen, 1981; Terrell, 1981). Krashen (1982) has made a distinction between subconscious and conscious language acquisition learning. He said that: "...acquisition differs from learning in two major ways: acquisition is slow and subtle, while learning is fast and, for some people, obvious" (p. 187). Acquisition is the picking up of first and second language with little or no formal instruction. It requires meaningful, natural interaction in the new language with a focus on understanding rather than on its form. Conscious learning depends upon formal instruction with the explicit teaching of rules and error correction. Krashen (1982) considers that the formal learning of language forms is of little importance in the development of communicative ability for most language learners, whereas active interaction in the language is and should be the major activity in the classroom. Since first language learners develop comprehension long before they speak, early listening is usually accompanied by some form of activity such as physical responses to instructions given in a new language with simple verbal commands and verbal responses.

Terrell (1977) and Krashen (1981) state that as the children acquire language, errors in grammar should be accepted and tolerated as they gain experience in communication and get much practice in creating new utterances within meaningful contexts. This is done through a classroom environment that: (a) focuses on the learners' language needs; (b) provides little error correction; (c) leaves learners' language production until they feel comfortable with comprehension and the utterances, having first internalized the language and its meaning; and (d) provides a positive acceptance of the language learners' native language. Krashen (1982) reiterates that the conditions in which "language acquisition" takes place best are when input is provided that is: (a) comprehensible, (b) interesting and/or relevant to the acquirer, (c) not grammatically sequenced, and (d) provided in sufficient quantity. In order for this approach to succeed, there is a need for low anxiety situations where the child is personally involved in free flowing classroom activities. In order to present English learners with a language acquisition environment, ESL educators need to create a language curriculum and texts that are interesting and meaningful to students. This curriculum is made up of students' experiences, interests, and teachers' observations of students' own interests and needs. Each activity provides the student with an opportunity to use language for what it was intended: a tool in communication (Krashen, 1981; Terrell, 1977).

Total Physical Response (TPR)

This approach was developed primarily by Asher (1965). His approach is based on the concept that second language acquisition can be accelerated through the use of the kinesthetic sensory system (Asher, 1977). Asher based his language acquisition theory on how children learn their first language in which the infant must first internalize a working understanding of the target language. Asher considered three critical elements of child language acquisition: (a) listening in advance of speaking; (b) the understanding of spoken language, which may be acquired when adults manipulate the physical behavior of the infants through commands; and (c) listening skills that may produce a "readiness" for the child to speak.

Many studies have been conducted in various languages to support Asher's learning strategy. Asher's studies showed that understanding the spoken language should be developed before speaking. And although the TPR cannot be considered a complete method, it is useful for both adults and children in the early stages of second language learning.

The TPR procedure may vary according to size of group, age, language proficiency level, and nature of the lesson, but there are several basic characteristics common to all lessons. These are: (a) understanding is developed before speaking, (b) new vocabulary is developed through the use of commands, (c) understanding is demonstrated through action, and (d) learners speak when they are ready. Asher proposes tolerance for learners' errors at the beginning stage because when proficiency increases, language usage is refined.

Suggestopedia

In the approach called "suggestopedia," Lozanov (1979) stated that learning involves the unconscious functions of the learner as well as the conscious functions. Recommended strategies include: (a) review done using traditional conversations, games, or plays; (b) presentation of new material introduced in the form of dialogues based on situations familiar to the students; (c) dialogues read by the teacher, while learners follow the text and engage in deep and rhythmic yoga breathing; and (d) engagement in interaction activities based on the dialogue. In this approach, learners may assume different identities through dramatic roles and puppetry. Students immerse themselves in the character being played. In dramatic play learners' unconsciousness can project itself into the creative effort, allowing them to feel freer to express their emotions and experiences. Long dialogues are presented in phases, with long spaces of silence and classical music. Therefore, the expansion of knowledge is accelerated further than would otherwise be expected.

This approach also emphasizes that students can learn much faster than they usually do by removing psychic tension (Lozanov,

1979). It stands to reason that a learner will retain more of what is learned and feel freer to bring more to a situation when the environment and learning conditions are relaxed and non-threatening. It is then that learners are able to go much further than previously thought; therefore, the removal of limits or inhibiting tension offers the second language learners the opportunity to seek and reach higher intellectual goals. Suggestopedia is not considered a method but a methodological strategy to be used as part of the ESL instructional program and part of other approaches.

Counseling-Learning

This approach is partly influenced by the cognitive-affective (humanistic and developmental) psychology. Counseling-Learning is an approach which emphasizes the humanistic side of language learning. It is an approach to second and foreign language teaching in which small or large groups are formed to create a language learning community. Curran (1972) claimed that the non-threatening counseling relationship provides the optimal environment for learning. In this approach the learners' personal feelings and reactions to language learning situations are an integral part of the learning process. During class sessions learners decide what they want to talk about. The teacher, taking on the role of "counselor," translates these topics into the target language which the learner initiates with a statement; then the counselor repeats the statement correctly to the other group. Each one advances independently in speaking the target language according to his/her abilities and is assisted when necessary. As the students become more advanced, more exact corrections are made, and special idiomatic expressions are supplied by the expert language counselor, much like an upward cyclical approach (from the simple to the more complex). This approach makes a difference in the students' relationship to the counselor and the group as they become more secure and independent in the one or more languages.

Language Experience Approach (LEA)

The language experience approach has been proposed as an initial reading program for English-speaking children in which students produce reading materials based on their own interests and language background (Van Allen & Allen, 1976). Learners recount stories and the teacher writes their stories. The learner-produced stories are used as reading material and language development activities. The LEA approach capitalizes on shared experiences as a pathway to developing English reading skills. Learners are introduced to the written form of language which they control orally. Motivation is high as students are more apt to recognize their own words in print. In ESL classrooms the learners' experiences and ideas are used as a means of developing communication skills in all four skills: listening, speaking, reading, and writing. The LEA approach integrates all four language skills in a wholistic manner. It has many advantages for LEP students: they see their own words transformed into writing and used as a basis for a lesson, and it strengthens their self-esteem and promotes a close working relationship between the teacher and the learners. It can be used both as a vehicle for individual instruction or group work. A strong relationship emerges when working with groups because they feel that they have made a worthy contribution to the group and their words and experiences are important since they can say and read it again and again.

Content-Based Approach

This instructional approach was designed using modified subject matter content to assist LEP students in the development of the academic language skills they need to participate successfully in the mainstream classroom. As Mohan (1986) stated:

> what is needed is an interactive approach which relates language learning and content learning, considers language as a medium of learning, and acknowledges the role of context in communication. Such an approach will not only be of value for students learning

through a second language, it will have implications for all language learners. And it will have implications for education in general. (p. 1-2)

A content-based approach seeks to develop both second language skills and academic concepts appropriate to the students' grade level. To achieve this goal the scope of instruction is broad enough to embrace the language and the concepts of content-area subjects. Teaching English is not an end in itself, but only a means to succeed in school (Saville-Troike, 1984). This instructional approach helps second language learners to: (a) strengthen language skills while acquiring specific concepts, (b) improved communication of subject matter, and (c) identification strategies, knowledge, and academic skills that are crucial for success in content-area subjects. This approach involves the incorporation of subject matter instruction appropriate to the students' age and grade level into a language development program. Subject-matter content is interwoven into language lessons, allowing language learners to focus on the content or meaning rather than on the structure of the language. Also, new information presented in these classes is often a catalyst for further academic and language learning. The motivation for language learning arises naturally as students become involved in understanding concepts of history, science, or mathematics. Mohan (1986) recommends a content-based curriculum in which the following characteristics are shown: (a) a developed framework of language and thinking skills which apply across the curriculum, (b) improved communication of subject matter, (c) identification of strategies for the development of language skills, and (d) identification of strategies for the development of thinking skills. ESL programs have welcomed this approach, sometimes calling it "sheltered English."

Eclectic Approach

The eclectic approach to language development encompasses a diversity of techniques and activities. The eclectic approach to ESL teaching incorporates the most appropriate or useful parts of all existing approaches, principles, and theories from the field of language teaching. The eclectic approach being proposed here is based on the following principles:

1. Second language learners bring a great deal of experience and knowledge to their language learning situation.
2. Learners' use of translation from native language to second language establishes a basis for communication.
3. Language learning should be taught in the target language whenever possible.
4. Language learning must be meaningful and interesting.
5. Subject-content enriches and provides a cognitive base to the language classroom.
6. Mimicry, memorization, and pattern practice may serve the needs in the classroom at the teacher's discretion.
7. Vocabulary acquisition should be used in meaningful contexts. Continuous appropriate usage will aid in vocabulary retention.
8. Reading and writing should not be delayed and should be incorporated in almost every ESL lesson.

ESL teachers have a wide selection of approaches available to meet the needs of the participating second language learners, and these teachers are in the best position to know which aspects of the various approaches will prove to be the most useful within the classroom setting and which will best complement their teaching style. Teachers, then, need to know all the existing approaches, theories, and practices of second language teaching and learning and to know the cognitive and linguistic characteristics of the students being served. It is then, after experimenting with these approaches and with materials that focus on specific language theories, that they make the decision to incorporate those strategies that learners seem to accept as well as demonstrate language and academic learning. This mixing, incorporating, choosing, and eliminating varies according to content language skills being emphasized and the level of proficiency of the learners.

Materials for Instruction

The ESL approaches recommended in the previous section require teacher development of curriculum, planning, and development of instructional materials. This section lists materials for instruction useful in teaching English to LEP learners.

1. *The Picture File.* Every classroom should contain a file of pictures to illustrate socio-cultural topics as well as to provide interesting, meaningful practice in the sounds, structures, and vocabulary of English. Pictures should be large enough to be seen by all learners. The pictures of individual objects or people should be as simple as possible.

2. *Charts.* Simple charts showing specific relationships (i.e., grammatical, semantic) are extremely valuable. For example, the use of verb tenses can be illustrated graphically by simple lines on a chart.

3. *Flash Cards.* Cards with individual words can be prepared and filed within the same categories and in the same order as the individual pictures. The cards should be about twelve inches long and four inches wide. Younger children can be asked to match cards and pictures as soon as they can read. They can also match the cards with words written on the blackboard or on a large cardboard.

4. *The Pocket Chart.* This simple teaching tool is an excellent device for dramatizing word order. It is easily made by taking a piece of cardboard or hard paper (about two feet in length by about one foot in height), and pinning (stapling or gluing) to it two narrow pockets about two inches high.

5. *The Flannel Board.* This simple device is excellent in presenting and practicing concepts, vocabulary, and grammatical structures. With younger students, it is useful in playing games or in dramatizing stories. Pictures or cutouts with a small piece of flannel glued to the back adhere easily to the flannel and permit the illustration and teaching of many concepts or structures.

6. *Games and Songs.* There are all kinds of language games and songs ranging from very simple to difficult ones which help give

practice in language while keeping the class lively and interesting. The type of song teachers will use will depend on the age, interests, and learning level of the students. Songs for children, for example, should contain a repetitive phrase where possible. Songs for intermediate levels and/or older students may have love, patriotism, home, and holidays as themes. Putting English words to favorite melodies from the students' countries is a very good way to motivate students to think.

7. *The Record Player.* Songs, dances, stories, plays, and other language learning materials can be found on records. Newer English textbooks are often accompanied by recordings of dialogues and many practice activities. Some include pauses for student repetition.

8. *The Language Laboratory.* Where the language laboratory exists, teachers should make every attempt to use it for meaningful purposes. For example, learners, especially children, like to hear a story several times. The language laboratory provides such opportunities offering the advantage of maintaining the same intonation, repeating it without tiring, and providing a uniform length of pause for student repetition.

9. *Real Objects.* A corner of the room or a large box on reserve should contain anything teachers can gather together to illustrate vocabulary, concepts or cultural concepts. Newspapers, menus, flags, maps, ticket stubs, cans, bottles, boxes, pieces of different kinds of cloth, wax flowers, dishes, and silverware, all are part of the objects in the ESL classroom.

References

Asher, J. J. (1965). Comprehension training: The evidence from laboratory and classroom studies. In H. Winitz (Ed.), *The comprehension approach to foreign language instruction* (pp. 187-219). Rowley, MA: Newbury House.

Asher, J. J. (1977). *Learning another language through actions: The complete teacher's guidebook.* San Jose, CA: Sky Oaks Productions.

Curran, C. (1972). Counseling-learning: In J. W. Oller & P. Richard-Amato (Eds.), *Methods that work* (pp. 146-175). Rowley, MA: Newbury House.

Krashen, S. (1981). *Second language acquisition.* Oxford, England: Pergamon.

Krashen, S. (1982). *Principles and practice in second language acquisition.* New York: Pergamon.

Lozanov, G. (1979). *Suggestology and outlines of suggestopedy.* New York: Gordon and Breach.

Mohan, B. A. (1986). *Language and content.* Reading, MA: Addison-Wesley.

Oller, J. W. & Richard-Amato, P. (1983). *Methods that work.* Rowley, MA: Newbury House.

Richards, J. C. & Rodgers, T. (1986). *Approaches and methods in language teaching.* London: Cambridge University Press.

Rigg, P. (1991). Whole language in TESOL. *TESOL Quarterly, 25*(3), 521-542.

Saville-Troike, M. (1984). What really matters in second language learning for academic achievement. *TESOL Quarterly, 18,* 199-219.

Terrell, T. D. (1977). A natural approach to second language acquisition and learning. *Modern Language Journal, 41,* 325-337.

Terrell, T. D. (1981). The natural approach in bilingual education. In California State Department of Education, *Schooling and language minority students: A theoretical framework* (pp. 117-146). Los Angeles, CA: Evaluation, Dissemination and Assessment Center, California State University.

Van Allen, R. & Allen, C. (1976). *Language experience activities.* Boston, MA: Houghton Mifflin.

Weaver, C. (1988). *Reading process and practice: From sociolinguistics to whole language.* Portsmouth, NH: Heinemann.

CHAPTER 8

The Development of English Listening and Speaking Skills

Listening and speaking play central roles in language acquisition and development. They also represent two of the most difficult components of the English language for ESL learners to acquire. Listening is the ability to understand speech. Speaking is the act of communicating through speech. Both are vitally important in human relations, international relations, and to academic and business success. In recent decades more research has been done in the areas of first and second language acquisition. Findings have influenced second language teaching and have resulted in the development of new methods which emphasize listening prior to speaking, reading and writing, especially in the initial stages of learning. This is in keeping with the changing social and political purposes for learning a second language. This chapter discusses the roles of listening comprehension and speaking in the English language development of LEP students as well as recommended instructional strategies.

Listening Comprehension

Listening comprehension is central to second language acquisition. In the last two decades it has become increasingly common to emphasize listening in the early stages of second language acquisition. Pedagogical theory tends to support the beneficial aspects of providing beginning ESL learners' "silent period" in their second language development (Krashen, 1981). Listening is an active and conscious process. Second language listeners construct meaning (as does the first language listener) through an interaction with the spoken text or the speaker, which involves using contextual clues, prior knowledge, and relying upon a variety of strategies to make sense of the incoming information (Chamot & O'Malley, 1988). Not only is listening comprehension important at the beginning stages of second language acquisition, it appears to be crucially important for advanced level learners as well (Dunkel, 1991).

Attentional factors during perceptual processing are fundamental for comprehension and can be expected to contribute to listening comprehension in second language learners. Rost (1990) suggests that second language listeners engage in the following processes while listening: (a) estimating the sense of lexical inferences, (b) constructing propositional meaning, (c) assigning a "base (conceptual) meaning" in the discourse, (d) assigning underlying links in the discourse, and (e) assuming a plausible intention for the speakers' utterances.   Listening comprehension is a function of the listener's basic information-processing ability and level of cognitive complexity. Listening comprehension is enhanced through repetition of the material by the speaker and the listener.   Listeners need to employ cognitive strategies if they are to function effectively.   Skillful listeners monitor their comprehension and infer the meaning of new words from context clues.   Chamot and O'Malley (1988) found that successful second language learners use the following three strategies in listening comprehension: (a) self-monitoring, (b) elaboration, and (c) inferring.

Classroom materials for listening comprehension should include those that emphasize strategies that convey factual or propositional information (a transactional purpose) as well as strategies to enhance social relationships (Richards, 1990). Figure 8.1 presents an example of a beginning level task in which listeners need to understand the message being conveyed to perform according to the factual information provided. The teacher will be giving the instructions and the students will perform the task. It is important to have richness and variety in listening activities and processes. In the classroom, in addition to conversation activities such as listening to pre-taped weather forecasts, songs, and radio announcements can add considerable interest to a lesson (Porter & Roberts, 1987).

Figure 8.1. Listen and Do It.

Can You Do This?
In the following examples students need to pay attention in order to listen and do what is asked.

1. Make a big house.
2. Put three windows in the house.
3. Put a red door on the house.
4. Color the house brown and green.
5. Make two trees beside the house.
6. Color them green.
7. Make red and yellow flowers in front of the house.
8. Make a sun in the sky.
9. Make a boy and a girl beside the tree.
10. Make grass around the house.

Speaking in the ESL Classroom

The main aspect of speaking is communication. Halliday (1978) suggested that communication takes place when there is sharing of experience, expression of social solidarity, decision-making, and planning. Spoken language is an important part of the identities of all participants, and the second language learner plays an active role in speaking the target language to communicate. Thus, context and opportunity play a critical role in how much and how often LEP students use the English language. Spoken language is the medium by which students demonstrate to teachers much of what they have learned (Cazden, 1988). Cazden identifies three functions of language: (a) the communication of propositional information, (b) the establishment and maintenance of social relationships, and (c) the expression of the speaker's identity and attitudes. Speaking allows individuals to express themselves concisely, coherently, and in a manner that suits all audiences and occasions. This ability to speak easily and well is important, because it facilitates interpersonal and public communication. The listening and speaking skills form a basis for developing skills in reading and writing. ESL students living in the United States or other English speaking countries have the advantage of a language-rich environment which teachers can draw upon. For those who do not have this advantage, providing it can be a major challenge.

At the beginning level, instruction and learning can be accomplished by teachers welcoming their students to class each day with simple greetings in English. If the room is too warm or too cool, teachers can ask students, in English, to open or to close the window, employing gestures, sketches on the blackboard, and demonstrations. The aim is to enable students to begin to understand and to speak English automatically, without having to "stop and think" or to perform laborious mental translations before responding to or in English.   Research suggests a "pre-speaking" period of second language instruction, delaying oral practice in early-stage learning. Dunkel (1991) cites authorities that suggest that learners who are required too early to speak are likely to suffer from "task overload" which probably inhibits language acquisition and the exercise and development of discrimination skills creates anxiety and encourages interference from the first language.

In the past ten years the area of speaking in ESL teaching has been re-examined and through the process many views and concepts were developed (Gary & Gary, 1981; Garton & Pratt, 1989). Views include: (a) the need for the learners' involvement, (b) for learners to self-monitor their speech, (c) the need for language materials to appeal to learners' cognitive involvement, and (d) the importance of meaning and contextualized practice. Meaningful communication is important and necessary for LEP students' mastery of English; they need effective language use to help them not just to survive but to succeed in an English speaking environment.   The 1990s has provided the environment   for   an   emphasis   on   communication,   on   oral comprehensibility,   making   it   of   critical   importance   to   provide instruction that enables students to become, not "perfect pronouncers" of English, but intelligible, communicative, confident users of spoken English for whatever purposes they need.

Let Students Do Most of the Talking

It is enjoyable for speakers to talk about subjects of interest, and, as English educators, teachers may like to discuss topics of interest to them. However, it is students who need speaking practice, not the teacher, and in order to learn the language, students must use and practice English in meaningful situations. Many language teachers are inclined to talk too much (Carruthers, 1987; Mockridge-Fong, 1979), and certain students, in order to avoid the hard work of learning, are skillful at "keeping the teacher talking" by asking endless questions. Teachers should not let students involve them in lengthy explanations, arguments, or lectures. The best and most valid answer to the question "Why do you say it that way in English?" is frequently, "Because that is the custom of the English language." The sooner the students realize that language habits derive from custom and usage rather than from logic, the sooner they will get down to the serious business of mastering a new set of language skills. As a general rule, we may say that the teacher should do no more than 25 percent of the talking in the class, and that students should be permitted to do 75 percent of the talking. The teacher should speak to model correct pronunciation which students need to hear in order to learn. The good teacher is like the conductor of an orchestra who directs the musicians. The teacher introduces a topic; then, by means of carefully planned activities, leads the class in numerous activities related to that topic. Often, the class responds as a group. Frequently, individual performers will be called upon to express their own point of view. The teacher insures that the interest is maintained, that there is a proper balance between all skills that are emphasized in the speaking activity.

Conversation

Speaking means that the teacher must first identify the kinds of situations which require effective communication and the kinds of speaking skills required by those situations (Richards, 1990). The most obvious and common situation requiring speech is conversation. Conversation may range from kindergartners talking out loud to themselves to sixth graders trading views on the school's hot-lunch program. Conversation is simply talking together about something of mutual interest. Effective conversation requires: (a) using language others can understand, (b) using an appropriate tone of voice, (c) expressing ideas and responses clearly, (d) listening to others, and (e) being aware of the body and facial cues of oneself and of others.

Conversation often leads to discussion. Although the two are quite similar, discussion usually involves some degree of problem solving; it is more formal than conversation. Discussion requires focusing on an agreed-on topic. Since there is a problem-solving orientation, discussion requires sticking to the subject while remaining sensitive to the responses of the other participants. If one speaker uses inappropriate language yet never realizes it, the discussion can break down. But if speakers are aware of and sensitive to verbal and nonverbal cues, they can modify their speaking to match the needs of the other participants. Effective discussion requires: (a) focusing on the topic–and staying there; (b) listening carefully; (c) participating as a speaker and as a listener; (d) providing reasons for attitudes and/or opinions; and (e) encouraging others to contribute to the discussion.

Pronunciation

The acquisition of good pronunciation in the target language is commonly held to be the most difficult of all tasks in second language learning. After the age of puberty, native pronunciation becomes more difficult to acquire. Various reasons have been offered in explanation of this phenomenon. For one thing, habits of using the speech organs in one's first language grow stronger with practice. For this reason, it is not recommended that adults spend a great amount of time trying to eliminate their accents, but rather that they strive for fluency, control of structure and, above all, understanding (Finocchiaro, 1989). In teaching all ages, pronunciation needs emphasis. Those errors which cause the learner to be misunderstood or not understood are the most important to correct. As the learner progresses, more emphasis can be put on achieving pronunciation which is not distracting.

Pronunciation is an integral part of communication, not an isolated drill. It is best learned through imitation and practice in situations that are of interest to the learner. Current perspectives on second language learners' involvement in the pronunciation learning/teaching process include an emphasis on speech awareness and self-monitoring, while the teacher becomes a facilitator, a coach and organizer of instructional activities, making certain that students have appropriate and adequate input on which to model their pronunciation.

Meaningful practice, especially speech activity experiences suited to the communication styles and needs of the learners' real life situations, is recommended. Research emphasizes that meaningful communication is needed for acquisition to occur (Cazden, 1988). Supervised practice needs to take into account the uniqueness of each ESL learner. Each second language learner will create his/her own personal pattern of spoken English, influenced by many personal and communicative strategies as well as the input of instruction.

Vocabulary

Vocabulary acquisition is an interactive process that includes the learners' cognitive processes as well as learning strategies (Brown and Perry, 1991; Nattinger, 1988). From the author's own experience with LEP students, it is felt that a good amount of vocabulary, with a minimum of structure, often makes for better English speakers, readers, and writers. It is generally accepted that the larger the number of words learners have mastered, the better their English comprehension is. There is tremendous variety in the vocabulary strategies employed by second language learners. Naiman, Fröhlich, Stern and Todesco (1978) list strategies that learners reported they used to develop their vocabulary in the second language. Among those strategies are: (a) preparing vocabulary lists, (b) learning words in context, and (c) practicing vocabulary. Naiman, Fröhlich, Stern, and Todesco indicated that students use a variety of strategies in practicing vocabulary. Those mentioned include: deliberately putting words into different structures in order to drill oneself, reading to reinforce vocabulary, playing games such as trying to think of words with the same ending, and repeating words to oneself. These strategies vary depending on the learners' needs, interests, and purpose for learning the particular lexicon. Many teachers think that LEP students' vocabulary can be improved by bombarding them with vocabulary lists and drills, usually carried out in isolation. Vocabulary learned in this way is often soon forgotten. Second language research indicates the need for relevant, contextualized input.

The English lexicon (words, meanings, derivation) needs to be learned and it needs to be taught. Teachers should be careful to choose techniques that contextualize word meanings best. Most important is the teacher's ability to arouse in learners a genuine interest in vocabulary to develop the skills and the curiosity that will guarantee the growth of every student's vocabulary far beyond the temporal limits of the ESL classroom.

Strategies for Developing Listening and Speaking Skills

Role play, problem solving, and magic tricks are recommended ESL strategies.

Role Play

Role play is an exercise where students are assigned fictitious roles from which they have to improvise some kind of behavior toward another's role characters in the exercise (Richard-Amato, 1988; Scarcella, 1987). In most role playing, as in the opening of a bank account, students may simply be assigned to play a role having a simulated situation rather than a real role to play. The two basic requirements for role play are improvisation and fictitious roles. Role play can be very simple and the improvisation highly controlled, or it can be very elaborate. Which tasks educators should choose is primarily a matter of learners' English proficiency. Certainly role play can be used in beginning classes as well as in advanced ones.

The format of a role play consists of three basic parts: the situation, the roles, and useful expressions. Occasionally, a pre-preparation with background knowledge is needed for advanced role play. The situation sets the scene and the plot, i.e., explains the situation and describes the task or action to be accomplished. Again, the task can be very simple, such as a telephone call, or very elaborate, as settling a complex business deal. The situation is a good place to introduce specific cultural information if that is part of the objective of a given role play. All characters should have fictitious names; this aids in the willing suspension of disbelief. It is recommended to include such information as personality, experience, status, personal problems and desires, and the like. A role can be very simple, merely a skeleton name and status or quite elaborate, but role descriptions should not be overly elaborate because then the playing of the role becomes a matter of clever acting and that is not the objective. On the contrary, it is inhibiting and counterproductive. Teachers want LEP students themselves to create the personality through hints of background or behavior. Useful utterances contain linguistic information, common expressions, phrases, and technical vocabulary (an efficient way to teach vocabulary). Grammar patterns which are necessary are also learned through role playing.

Input and incorporation of background knowledge is essential. It is no good at all to ask students to act out roles which demand general knowledge they do not possess. For example, in order to act out a school board meeting on open classrooms, a town meeting on local industrial pollution, or a newspaper interview on the problems of AIDS, second language learners must have subject matter information prior to the role play. It need not be complicated at all–a short reading assignment, a lecture by the teacher, a guest lecture, or film. But some source of knowledge is necessary or the role play will not meet the objectives for which it was planned.

Problem-Solving Activities

These exercises are just what they sound like; the students are presented with a problem, and they respond to the problem using different strategies such as small group discussion or step by step group discussion. Figure 8.2 is an example of a popular exercise being currently used in many ESL classrooms. Through problem solving, students can examine causes of problems, identify solutions, analyze problems, and decide on a course of action (Little & Greenberg, 1991).

Figure 8.2. A Camping Trip

You are going on a three-day camping trip up in the mountains. You will carry everything you need for the three days on your back. Since you are going into the mountains, it will be cold. This kind of trip is called a pack trip because you walk and carry everything you take with you on your back in a bag called a "pack." You have decided that you can't carry more than 20 pounds on your back comfortably. You made a list of things you want to take with you, but they add up to more than 20 pounds. Now you have to read your list and include only the most important items. Remember they cannot add up to more than 20 pounds, including the pack. Also remember that you will not see anyone for the three days and you must include everything you need in order to survive.

Problem: You must come up with a list of items and be sure you add up weights so they don't total more than 20 pounds. You must be able also to tell why you chose each item.

Magic Tricks

Since children and adults are fascinated by magic tricks, and since the tricks described here require practice, repetition, and variation in language use, this strategy for learning can be effective and memorable. It is a good idea for the teacher to first explain the trick, using the appropriate materials and a volunteer from the group. The teacher visually demonstrates, naming materials and actions. Figure 8.3 presents an example of magic tricks. After everyone is astonished the teacher asks several students to write the process on the board.

Figure 8.3. Magic Birthday

Ask one of the students to:

1. Multiply his or her age by three,
2. Add six to the result,
3. Divide by three,
4. Then, two must be taken away (subtract two)
5. The result will be the age of the learner!

The Video Cassette and the Video Camera

Both the video cassette and the video camera provide teachers and students a free and relaxed learning environment to make the language learning experience varied, interesting, relevant, and enjoyable. Using the video cassette, imagination, creativity, and the development of personal skills can flourish. The use of this media provides: (a) the motivation achieved by basing lessons on attractive informative content material; (b) the exposure of a varied range of authentic speech, with different registers, accents, intonation, rhythms, and stresses; and (c) language used in the context of real situations, which add relevance and interest to the learning process. Activities such as vocabulary development, writing from a character's point of view, or stopping the tape in the middle of the action to predict the outcome are examples of practices which work extremely well with both film and video tape.

One recommended activity is the production of a class news program (Malu, 1991). Malú (1991) described the strategy as follows:

> Extending over a period of several weeks, students begin this unit by observing television news programs, noting not just the news stories but also how the broadcasters present their stories, the lead-in lines used, even the commercials which appear. After several class discussions students begin to write their own news stories, engaging in library research and the collection of empirical data where necessary, seeking interviews with classmates or other school officials where appropriate, and finally writing their stories. Next, they prepare the background props, maps, headings, photos, whatever may be appropriate to their story. On the day of the videotaping, there is tremendous activity in the classroom. Each student realizes the seriousness of this project and the weeks of preparation finally become very real. (p. 8)

Other Activities

Almost everything that goes on in the classroom helps develop language, especially listening and speaking skills. The following list of activities can be developed into structured activities for enhancing language.

1. Pictures: (a) pictures arranged by classification or groups; (b) giving titles to pictures; (c) picture dictionary made from magazine pictures; (d) using language machines with noun and verb picture cards.
2. Games: (a) teacher-made games to reinforce vocabulary growth; (b) teaching choral speaking, jingles, songs; (c) acting out plays; (d) pantomiming (teacher tells child what to do); (e) using a telephone prop and acting out conversations; (f) playing a verbal game called "Where am I?" Child identifies place (such as dentist's office through pictures).
3. Use of classroom as a source of language: (a) teach names of furniture and equipment; (b) teach directions in room (front, back, middle top shelf, bottom, inside, on top); (c) use clock and

calendar to teach time, months, days, holidays, weather; (d) change bulletin boards frequently to arouse interest; (e) have collections of things in rooms; (f) use records and tapes, films, filmstrips, puppets.

4. Listening activities: (a) read aloud to students every day; read interesting news to them (i.e., what happened to a famous person, an anecdote) (b) Listening to the news is a good opportunity to help students develop listening comprehension.

5. Action routines: Each pupil learns to follow the directions of the teacher, using the imperative form. Figure 8.4 presents a list of daily classroom routines:

Figure 8.4. Classroom Daily Routines

Stand up.	Make an x.	Tear the paper.
Come here.	Underline.	Push the ____.
Go to the door.	Circle.	Bend the wire.
Open the door.	Cross out.	Fill the cup.
Turn on the light.	Shake hands.	Cut the ____.
Go to the window.	Pick up.	Cover the ____.
Raise your hands.	Take the ____.	Empty the ____.
Put your hands on the _____.	Give me the __.	Ring the bell.
Clap your hands.	Put back the __.	Feel the ____.
Get your book.	Point to the ___.	Hide the ____.
Sit down.	Write your name.	Erase the board.
Go to the back of___.	Draw a picture.	
Close the door.		

There are many different ways to create listening comprehension and speaking experiences. ESL teachers use a variety of total contexts, integrating basic skills with content that is interesting and meaningful to students. The extent to which teachers are successful may well depend upon their ability to recognize that teaching must include the learners' active participation, requiring them to choose among relevant lexical and syntactical content. The teacher's role is to encourage active use of the forms they teach.

References

Brown, T. S. & Perry, F. L. Jr. (1991). A comparison of three learning strategies for ESL vocabulary acquisition. *TESOL Quarterly, 25*(4), 655-670.

Carruthers, R. (1987). Teaching pronunciation. In M. H. Long & J. C. Richards (Eds.), *Methodology in TESOL* (pp. 191-199). Rowley, MA: Newbury House.

Cazden, C. (1988). Classroom discourse: The language of teaching and learning. Portsmouth, NH: Heinemann.

Chamot, A. U. & O'Malley, M. (1988). *Learner strategies for listening comprehension in English as a second language.* Paper presented at the American Educational Research Association, Annual Meeting, New York.

Dunkel, P. (1991). Listening in the native and second/foreign language: Toward an integration of research and practice. *TESOL Quarterly, 25*(3), 431-457.

Finocchiaro, M. (1989). *English as a second/foreign language.* Englewood Cliffs, NJ: Prentice-Hall.

Garton, A. & Pratt, C. (1989). *Learning to be literate: The development of spoken and written language.* Oxford: Basil Blackwell.

Gary, J. & Gary, N. (1981). Caution. Talking may be dangerous to your linguistic health. *IRAL, 19*, 1-14.

Halliday, M. A. K. (1978). *Language as social semiotic: The social interpretation of language and meaning.* Baltimore: University Park Press.

Krashen, J. (1981). *Second language acquisition and second language learning.* Oxford: Pergamon.

Little, L. W. & Greenberg, I. A. (1991). *Problem solving. Developing critical thinking and communication skills.* Reading, MA: Addison-Wesley.

Malu, K. (1991). *Technology in the ESL classroom.* Unpublished Paper.

Mockridge-Fong, S. (1979). Teaching the speaking skill. In M. Celce-Murcia & L. McIntosh (Eds.), *Teaching English as a second or foreign language* (pp. 90-100). Cambridge, MA: Newbury House.

Naiman, N., Fröhlich, M., Stern, H., & Todesco, A. (1978). The good language learner. *Research in Education,* No. 7. Toronto: Ontario Institute for Studies in Education.

Nattinger, J. (1988). Some current trends in vocabulary teaching. In R. Carter & M. McCarthy (Eds.), *Vocabulary and language teaching* (pp. 62-82). London: Longman Group.

Porter, D. & Roberts, J. (1987). Authentic listening activities. In M. H. Long & J. C. Richards (Eds.), *Methodology in TESOL* (pp. 177-187). Rowley, MA: Newbury House.

Richard-Amato, P. A. (1988). *Making it happen. Interaction in the second language classroom. From theory to practice.* New York: Longman.

Richards, J. C. (1990). *The language teaching matrix.* New York: Cambridge University Press.

Rost, M. C. (1990). *Listening in language learning.* New York: Longman.

Scarcella, R. C. (1987). Socio-drama for social interaction. In M. H. Long & J. C. Richards (Eds.), *Methodology in TESOL* (pp. 208-214). Rowley, MA: Newbury House.

CHAPTER 9

The Development of English Literacy Skills

The function of language is communication. Comprehension is the goal of all communication. In the language modes of speaking and writing, comprehension means understanding the message well enough to compose it clearly. In the language modes of listening and reading, comprehension means interpreting the message clearly enough to understand its meaning. Consequently, reading instruction focuses on getting meaning from text; writing instruction focuses on creating meaning in text. In the general sense, reading and writing development is called literacy. Literacy is the sharing of recreational and functional messages through language. English as a second language learners need to be engaged in both recreational and functional literacy activities in order to expand and enrich their English language skills. The purpose of this chapter is to define literacy, describe its characteristics and components as well as to list successful literacy development strategies for learners for whom English is their second or foreign language.

Literacy: A Definition

Literacy has different dimensions and functions. The term literacy has various meanings depending upon the classifications of the educational and the worldly experiences of each individual (Goodman, Goodman & Hood, 1989; Wells, 1990). Authorities have identified three broad categories of literacy: functional, cultural, and critical. Functional literacy is often related to basic writing (coding) and reading (decoding) skills that allow people to produce and understand simple texts. For English as a second language (ESL) students, functional literacy means providing them opportunities to attain high-level literacy skills. It may include emphasis on native language literacy as well as in the second language. Cultural literacy emphasizes the need for shared experiences and points of reference to fully comprehend texts. What a text means depends on what second language readers bring to the reading or writing act, and what second language learners bring depends largely on their cultural background, educational background, experiences, and ideology. The culture of ESL students influences their reading understanding and their writing performance, it provides a foundation of shared knowledge and traditions. Critical literacy identifies the political component inherent in reading and writing. To be "literate" means to be able to recognize the social and ideological nature of the text. Second language learners need to be able to identify the ideological elements used in texts and the writer's ideological perspective.

Literacy represents a level of reading and writing that enables second language learners to function in an English-speaking society. However, there is no agreement among authorities about what is an appropriate reading and writing level of literacy. Some authorities consider functional literacy to be between a fourth and eighth grade reading level as the appropriate level to indicate when individuals are functionally literate. Therefore, the ESL program needs to provide a language program that focuses on preparing students to function in an English reading and writing literate environment. Since ESL students are evaluated on literacy levels, there is a need to provide them with a recreational and functional curriculum that will create in them the purpose and motivation to progress in reading and writing in the second language. But describing writing's functionality is not an easy task. There are no developmental writing performance measures by grade level. This is to say that writing is not assessed frequently enough to identify writing levels for each grade. Also, ESL learners bring some literacy development in their native language that may not be reflected in their reading and writing proficiency in the second language.

The Language, Reading, and Writing Connection

During the last decade there has been a shift away from the

popular theories of reading, writing, and oral speech as separate entities, toward a holistic approach where language, reading, and writing are viewed as interrelated and interdependent. Sociolinguistic multilateral thinking has replaced limited behaviorist psycholinguistic theory and more emphasis is being placed on child centered, experience-based critical thinking instructional activities.

The controversy on the apparent dependence of reading upon oral language processing and knowledge structures appears to have developed in the 1980s as a result of educators' concerns arising from curriculum development issues (Resnick, 1986; Mayher, 1990). The question arose: What do we teach first, reading or oral language? Additionally it was asked: can a child be taught to read if his/her oral language development and knowledge structures are not in the normal academic range? Wells (1986), Bissex (1980), and Donaldson (1978) have all helped to offer answers to these questions. They posit that language is learned holistically. Oral language processing influences and interacts with reading and the knowledge structures. Thus, the question about which to teach first is irrelevant. Additionally, the knowledge about comprehension, composing, and the interrelationship between reading and writing have offered further evidence to suggest that there can be no linear path to meaningful development in reading and writing (Bissex, 1980; Smith, 1990). Strickland and Morrow (1993) have stated that oral language supports children's efforts towards literacy, and this oral language need not be fully developed for reading and writing to begin.

Although the above topic is still quite controversial, the importance of this issue today is of little relevance due to the findings of the similarities between reading, writing, and oral language development (Bissex, ₁980; Mayher, 1990; Resnick, 1986; Wells, 1986). The language process shares a variety of characteristics which Dickinson (1987) has identified in four types of relationships between oral language, reading, writing, and response to literature. The first is a dependence upon language-processing capabilities. To the extent that special abilities for language learning are involved in acquiring oral language, those same abilities might be necessary for literacy (Wyner, 1989; Verhoeven, 1987). The second is an interdependence of knowledge structures. Oral language is interdependent with the control of knowledge structures necessary for reading and writing (Hirsch, 1987). The third type of relationship is the support of acquisition of literacy with speech. Small group work and conversation provide excellent arenas for expanding the language/literacy relationship (Wells, 1986; Mayher, 1990). The fourth type of relationship is an independence of the different modalities. With proper experiences, children will be able to develop their own spelling and punctuation systems once they have learned some modality-specific information such as letters of the alphabet (Stevens & Slavin, 1991). Dickinson (1987) has stated that those abilities that are used for oral language are also the same ones necessary for developing written abilities. Donaldson (1978) discussed four types of relationships between oral language and reading, writing, and responses to literature. These are: (a) dependence upon language-processing capacities, (b) interdependence of knowledge structures, (c) support of acquisition of literacy with speech, and (d) independence of the different modalities. These relationships offer a view of comprehension as a phenomenon operating separately within oral language, reading, and writing as well as facilitating comprehension across modalities.

The activities of language, reading, and writing share both exact and similar language processing capacities beyond the simplistic though worthwhile assumption that all language and literacy development involves a communication purpose (Bissex, 1980; Donaldson, 1978; Hansen-Strain, 1987). These exact and similar characteristics are evidenced in the struggles and successes of learners as they attempt to embrace a new language or culture. For example, research focusing on successful second language acquisition based upon acquired levels of first language proficiency reveals that skills learned in support of one aspect of language/literacy assist in the acquisition of related tasks even when applied within the context of the new language (Hansen-Strain, 1987; Royer & Marlo, 1991; Wyner, 1989).

There is a strong connection between language development, reading, and writing. The better students are at using language, the more successful they will be at reading and writing the language. Students need a strong language foundation that includes a basic vocabulary, a reasonable range of knowledge about the world around them, and the ability to talk about their knowledge. Reading and writing are processes in which information from the text and the knowledge passed by the reader interact to produce new meaning.

Because the various language modes are so inextricably bound up with one another, it is almost impossible to teach one in isolation from the others. Oral and written language develop simultaneously, each facilitating and supporting learners' understanding of the other. Students learn written language by interacting with other learners and users in reading and writing situations, by exploring print on their own, and by observing other individuals using language for their communicative purposes.

Authentic language is holistic. Children learn letter-sound relations by reading real books and writing their own stories; they learn how to spell through exposure to words in their reading; they understand how adjectives work by encountering those employed by authors and by using those they need in their own writing. Thus, at the same time that they are learning language, they are learning through language and learning about language itself. In an integrated language classroom, there are no separate listening, speaking, reading, and writing activities. The fact that they use authentic language in the classroom means that their use of language is integrated. Children learn about reading and writing by listening to books read to them. They also learn about reading and writing by listening and talking to their peers and teachers about the books they have read or when they share the writing they have composed.

Reading in a Second Language

Reading is a process of constructing meaning. As readers pass through the words on a page of text they are engaged in an intentional activity. That is, they have a reason for reading. Weaver (1988) defined reading as "the process of constructing meaning through the dynamic interaction (transaction) among the reader's existing knowledge, the information suggested by the written language, and the context of the reading situation." Constructing meaning includes understanding the information in the text as well as changing the knowledge used to understand the text in the first place. Readers need to be actively involved in the act of reading and interested in the content being read. Readers need a purpose for reading. Readers' purposes for reading will significantly influence not only the strategies they use but how much they will remember of the context read. A

good definition of the reading process is summarized by Williams &
Capizzi-Snipper (1990). They said:

> ...as the eyes pause at points in the text, word clusters enter a
> temporary storage area that we can call "short-term memory." They
> are held here for a fraction of a second while a cognitive process
> evaluates whether they are useful to the reader's purpose for
> processing the text.
>
> If they are deemed useful, they go into what we can call
> "working memory" where the actual construction of meaning
> appears to take place. The entire cluster is interpreted as a unit, and
> the potential meaning of the unit is matched against a broad set of
> logical relationships and internal representations of reality stored
> more or less permanently in "long-term memory". The meaning is
> potential until the matching process is completed because it exists
> only as a hypothesis of what the unit may actually mean. For
> ambiguous sentences, such as "Jim put the toy in the box on the
> shelf", readers will have two models to match the input against, and
> they will rely on the context to match the correct one to a single
> meaning....
>
> Once meaning is constructed through hypothesis testing, the
> cluster itself is purged to accommodate another incoming one. The
> first proposition may be stored immediately in long-term memory if
> is complete, or it may be stored temporarily in working memory if it
> is incomplete, to wait processing of the newly arrived word cluster.
> (p. 19)

Reading comprehension is not a linear process; successful readers
use the words in the pages as cues to formulate a representation of the
whole text. Clark & Clark (1977) and Smith (1972), among others,
mentioned that people do not look at every word on the page. Instead,
readers process lines of text into clusters of three to seven words,
depending on their verbal fluency and the difficulty of the text.
Successful readers skip sentences, read sentences backward, and loop
back from one sentence to an earlier one. Reading is not a process of
merely pronouncing words accurately with the teacher correcting
readers when they make mistakes. Reading in the second language
must take LEP students from the isolated view of reading as a
decoding process into reading as a holistic act. In a successful ESL

program reading for comprehension includes the following functions:

1. Readers must construct **purposes for reading**. Why are ESL readers reading a given selection? Only by developing purposes will readers be able to gain the appropriate kind of information and enjoyment while reading. The purpose may just be to find a specific piece of information, for example, in the directions for using a personal computer. Or the purpose may be to get the main idea in a newspaper editorial. Reading is goal directed and readers can utilize texts in various ways. The readers' individual goals influence the reading process. By establishing a goal, students are able to activate prior knowledge to generate hypothesis and formulate expectations which will guide their reading comprehension.

2. Readers must activate relevant **background/prior knowledge**. The knowledge a reader brings to the printed page affects the comprehension of the text.

3. Readers must allocate attention in order to **focus on major content** and not on less important content. Given our purposes for reading some information will be important, and other information will not be important, depending on the purpose of the reader. Time and effort would be wasted if readers did not direct their attention to the major or important content in order to make sense of the text. ESL teachers may use specific activities to guide students in identifying the major content in a reading text, for example, comparing and contrasting, cause and effect.

4. Readers must critically **evaluate** the content of the text. They must determine if the information presented is internally consistent. They must also check to see if the text information is consistent with their own prior knowledge and with general knowledge.

5. Readers must **monitor** ongoing activities to see if they are actually comprehending the text.

6. Readers must make and test **inferences** of many kinds. Readers are constantly filling in gaps and making assumptions while they read. Interpreting, predicting, and arriving at conclusions are all part of the process of reading for meaning. Readers need to focus on those inferences that will help them critically to analyze the content presented in the text. It is easy to make incorrect or

inaccurate inferences for a number of reasons. For example, an author might deliberately mislead us in order to set up a surprise ending to a story. Or we might develop an interpretation that fits all the facts up to a certain point but later come across a fact that does not fit. This set of functions helps to show just how complex the process of reading really is; it is even more complex if the reading is done in a second language.

7. Readers must **select** reading strategies that help them to understand what they read. Strategies are essential in the comprehension of texts. Students need to develop awareness of using reading strategies according to text level of difficulty or facility. Students need to develop strategies to know when to skip for more points, when to scan for particular information, when to read quickly or slowly, carefully or curiously, silently or aloud. The ESL teacher can help students select appropriate strategies such as problem-solving (If I don't understand the passage what can I do to be able to get its main content?), high level analysis (How am I able to separate the main ideas presented?), critical thinking (What do I need to know before reading this selection?), and even syllogistic reasoning (Is it really necessary to read this text?).

The process of teaching reading in English to LEP students is in many ways similar to teaching reading in the native language. But educators need to be aware of students' linguistic knowledge, home and community language as well as cultural background to provide content that is relevant and interesting. Instructional strategies and reading content should be examined in terms of aiming reading instruction for effective comprehension.

Writing a Second Language

Typically, students are taught to write after they have learned to read. Students initially practice writing the alphabet, then individual words, later these individual words are combined into paragraphs, and so on. This writing involves a heavy emphasis on rules and structure. When writing instruction follows reading instruction, it suggests that the language modes are distinct and different and that writing is built on reading. But all language activities are essentially similar, whether listening, speaking, reading, or writing. These four language areas are social actions to make requests, supply information, make assertions, or ask and answer questions. Learning to write is no longer regarded as a mechanical process where students work on isolated grammatical codes but is instead understood to be a complex human activity embedded with cognitive and social relationships. Instruction in writing has changed: writers are motivated to compose their own stories and ideas, writers write for a variety of audiences and purposes, draft, revise while their writing is in process, arrange for peers to respond to one another's writing, and progress through multiple drafts of their works.

Limited English proficient students develop writing skills through interaction with peers and teachers as well as through content, purpose, and structure of the oral and written tasks. These students need to feel that their writings are valued by the school, by parents and by the community as a whole. In addition, for students to become competent and proficient writers in English language skills, writing must be seen as "an interrelated holistic entity" in which all four areas (listening, speaking, reading, and writing) are presented in meaningful, interesting, and interactive contexts. Furthermore, children from cultures where the language spoken differs from that in the host country may appear to be developmentally delayed, learning disabled, or mentally handicapped in school. These children must learn not only grammar, vocabulary, and curriculum content but also new functions of language. It is these students who must be encouraged even more than others to develop their own language experience stories in creative ways so that they will want to share their ideas and write about their interests in the target language.

Students like to have an audience when they are learning to produce meaningful written language, and their first audience is often themselves and their teacher. Written language, like spoken language, must be exchanged in order to give it a purpose. Research indicates that writing, like speaking, is almost always directed toward an audience whose expectations shape the form and content of the message, making interaction an integral element of the process. As writers write and rewrite they approximate more closely the intended meaning and the form with which to express meaning. Also, research on writing points out the importance of the role of the teacher in the writing act. The teacher should: (a) be an adviser and critic, (b) help students clarify their own thinking, and (c) help the writer communicate the intended meaning to others.

The Writing-as-Process Model

In this model, writers are taught how to identify and investigate a topic, identify a readership and develop a piece of writing in a manner that reflects the fact that writing is a fundamentally dynamic process. The instruction focuses on equipping writers with the skills, knowledge, attitude, and habit of writing clearly to an audience (i.e., the teacher, themselves, the other students, their parents) for a specific purpose. It is neither teacher centered or student centered. The stages are:

Planning. Unless a topic has been assigned, the first problem many writers face is that of what to write about. Choosing a topic of interest and importance is central to planning. But planning does not stop once the writer has decided what to write about and has begun to put words down. Writers are actively engaged in planning at all stages of producing a text. They think of the ideas they want to express, gathering materials from external sources.

Drafting. Drafting is the act of putting thoughts down as written words. Other terms for the same act are writing, recording, and translating. Drafting is extremely complex because there are so many different elements the writer must consider at the same time. These range from concrete and relatively straightforward elements, such as spelling and punctuation, to highly abstract elements, such as clarity and the perspective of the audience.

Revising. Revising is the process of making changes in the text and of developing new thoughts about it. Revising often begins with the writer's reviewing the words he/she has drafted to see if they are conveying the intended message. Writers may make minor revisions, such as adding a new phrase, or they may make major revisions, such as reorganizing the flow of ideas or adding several new sections. Revising gives writers the opportunity to reshape and restructure their work.

Editing. Editing is the process of making corrections and adjustments, often rather minor ones, to prepare the work to be read by others. Editing and revising are similar in that both involve the making of changes. Editing, however, is usually more a matter of polishing than of basic reshaping. For example, editing may include correcting the spelling, grammar, capitalization, and punctuation in a piece of writing.

Publishing. Publishing involves making the work public or accessible to others. Usually, people think of publishing in the sense that a newspaper, book, or magazine is published. Publishing may be much simpler than that, however. The text may be recopied, typed, or otherwise made more legible. It may also be read aloud to an audience or shared in other ways.

As shown above, the writing process is complex and multifaceted. Although it is said that it includes different sub-processes, these sub-processes overlap. For example, as discussed above, revision and editing overlap in the sense that both involve making changes in the text. Also, the writer can move freely back and forth between subprocesses. For example, the writer may move from drafting to revising and then back to drafting again. The process involves idea formation, editing revision, composition, and re-composition as the writer develops the piece. This model is viable to ESL writers whose limited mastery of written and spoken English can make it frustrating to learn writing through the "rules first" method. The writing-as-process model includes focus on the elements of structure and style as well as punctuation and grammar.

Pragmatic Writing

Writing is a highly personal activity and students need to express themselves in written form. Writing is also a social action, carried out with the purpose of accomplishing a particular social function such as transmitting information or applying for a job or writing a letter expressing a particular concern. Writing is used as a tool of expression. This is an important function of using writing in the second language curriculum. Students need opportunities to see writing as a social tool. For example, if they need to get information on recreational parks, they should write a letter requesting a list of locations of these parks and specific recreational services provided. If students notice that the community does not provide enough safety devices, they should be able to write a letter to the Mayor or other city officials of the safety needs in their community. In this sense, writing is an interactive process; it is not a classroom dictation or form-filling task, an information report exercise, or any other classroom copying exercise. Teachers must focus on the purpose, the intention (content and topics), the audience or who is responding to the written work, and the final sharing and editing of students' products. Teachers guide students focusing on their interests, abilities, concerns, but more importantly on their social writing needs. For second language composers, writing is a cultural event in terms of the audience and the content (topics). Teaching and learning strategies derive from a "holistic approach" for literacy instruction. Such an approach values second language learners' background knowledge and strengths in developing discovery and inquiry learning modes.

Pragmatic writing is reactive rather than structured instruction. Therefore, when using writing pragmatically, the main concerns are: (a) Why do students need to write? (b) What type of information would they need to communicate, and (c) What writing medium is the most appropriate? These questions reflect students' self-perception within a social and cultural context, the content of printed materials as well as the second language learners' background knowledge which interacts with reading and writing tasks. However, in providing students with a challenging, interesting literacy environment, teachers need to be aware of second language learners' mastery (grammar, syntax, functions) and guide them wisely, helping them to improve orthographic and graphophonemic systems. It is expected that the more students write, the better developed their grammar, speaking, and reading will become. In summary, it can be said that second language learners need to practice product and pragmatic writing. These are interactive processes that occur in every ESL classroom on a regular basis. To be able to produce successful writers, ESL teachers need to emphasize the following:

1. Provide sufficient time for students to write frequently and for varied purposes.
2. Provide writing activities for students with opportunities to use a process/product approach (pre-writing, drafting, revising, editing) as well as pragmatic writing (letters, resumes).
3. Give students opportunities to select their own topics so that they become personally invested in their writing.
4. Encourage students to share their writing with classmates, as well as to respond to each other's work in constructive ways.
5. Encourage students to make reading-writing connections so that

their favorite authors become their writing teachers.

6. Give students opportunities to "publish" their work so that their writing is treated as literature.
7. Model the writing process and share their product with the class.

Literacy Instructional Strategies

Literacy in the second language needs to integrate the four communication skills and structure its content and instructional materials to facilitate meaningful learning. Learning to read reinforces the writing process and vice versa. Children who are learning to read and write in a second language bring to the process not only background knowledge of the multilevel cue system in a language but also a multifaceted array of personal variables that impact on literacy as a meaningful activity. The following instructional strategies recognize this integrative literacy development approach.

Reading Aloud to ESL Students

Increasing the proportion of students who read widely and with evident satisfaction ought to be as much a goal of reading instruction as increasing the number who are competent readers. An essential step in meeting that goal is providing students ready access to books that are interesting to them. An important activity for building the knowledge required for eventual success in reading is reading aloud to students. There is no substitute for a teacher who reads good stories to children. It stimulates the appetite of students for reading, provides a model of skillful oral reading, and provides background knowledge for speaking activities. It is a practice that should continue throughout the grades. In all content areas but especially during the communication arts class, reading aloud helps students to focus on the meaning being expressed through the printed pages. To provide for reading aloud requires that: (a) the daily schedule include a period where the teacher reads aloud, selecting from a variety of material (fiction, non-fiction, poetry, short stories, plays); (b) the classroom be equipped with a well-stocked library representing the best in children's literature; (c) schools encourage parents of young children to read aloud at home, using literature, newspapers, magazines, among others.

Think Aloud Activities

Think aloud activities are those used by the teacher to provoke students to engage in an oral discussion of an idea, an issue, or merely answer a question based on a previous reading of a text. This task probes the respondent to think so as to supply a response, and it directs that respondent to think about a particular topic. Questions can get students to think and respond in a way that stretches their comprehension abilities, current knowledge, and language ability. For example, through the use of questioning strategies, teachers can encourage students to check the comprehension and application of facts associated with written texts. Thinking aloud encourages critical thinking and language development by facilitating the intellectual process by which students integrate past experiences into new learning experiences. A classification system provides teachers opportunities to formulate questions in various levels of cognitive processes. For example, Bloom's (1954) categories of knowledge, comprehension, application, analysis, synthesis and evaluation have been used extensively in restructuring different levels of questions. Teachers also restructure closed questions (yes/no) into open questions (wh-form) to increase responses and direct students to expand discourse on the topic of discussion. (See Figure 9.1.)

Whatever thinking aloud techniques are used, teachers need to develop the following strategies: (a) focus on students' attitude of the learning material at a particular cognitive level, (b) help students extend thoughts at the same cognitive level or raise them to the next cognitive level, (c) expand question focus and encourage all students to talk, and (d) maintain appropriate classroom atmosphere.

Figure 9.1 provides examples of thinking aloud questions integrating different levels of difficulty. These activities can be done by the whole class or the teacher may want to group them by areas of interest or difficulty. They may be based on an assigned reading or on common space information. They may be answered orally or in written format.

Figure 9.1. Thinking Aloud Questions

Synthesis
How   would you compare_____ to _____?
How   can you prove_____to _____?
When   could _____be used suitably?
Analysis
What   could be added or combined with _____   to make a new _____?
What   is another way to _____?
How   could you design or use _____in a new way?
Application
What   are the parts or features of ____ _____?
How   is _____related to _____?
Why/How   is _____?
How   can you use _____to solve the problem of _____?
Factual Information
What   can you say about _____?
How   can you discuss _____in (quantity)_____of   words?
Which   is the best answer to this question about it _____?
Which   comes first, _____or _____?
How   can you arrange _____in the right order?
What is _____?
How/Where is_____used?
When/How did_____happen?

Based on B. Bloom's (1956) *Taxonomy of Educational Objectives.*

The Language Experience Approach

Typically, students describe their own knowledge and experiences as the teacher records them in writing. The "story" is then read aloud to students while pointing to the words. Students read the story aloud as a whole, in groups, or individually. Students then receive the typed or printed story to develop other related exercises. The language experience approach provides many advantages to children who are reading in a second language because interests and personal experiences are highly meaningful to students. Thus, learning to read is easier and more enjoyable when reading materials match the language patterns and speaking vocabulary of the readers. Many objects, experiences, and ideas can provide stimuli for oral language and lead to the dictation of the stories. When a child or a group dictates a story, discussion should flow naturally with the teacher participating as one member of the group, not as the dominant member. Most important is that the teacher encourages students to talk rather than structuring the session around teacher talk. The teacher should not represent an autocratic figure who asks the questions and gives the right answers but rather a contributor to the discussions that take place in the classroom. For example, after going on a trip to the zoo, students in a junior high school dictated the story that appears in Figure 9.2 to the teacher.

Figure 9.2.

A Trip to the Bronx Zoo

What did we see at the Bronx Zoo? We saw the following animals in the zoo: monkeys, zebras, lions, seals, bears, and tigers. The monkey was funny, he made us laugh. Zebras are beautiful and have black lines. The polar bears are very white and big. Going to the zoo was a wonderful experience.

This activity will bring other related activities such as grouping students to gather information on a particular animal, collecting stories about animals, or writing about domestic versus wild animals.

Cloze Activities for Vocabulary Development

This procedure is a technique that asks readers to anticipate meaning from context and to supply previously deleted words from a printed passage. Usually every fifth word is deleted on the assumption that every fifth word in a text can be predicted from context. However, when the cloze is used for instruction, there is no need to delete every fifth word, only those words students need to practice. Students fill them in (orally or in writing). This gives the teacher a rough idea of how well the text is understood. There are several exercises that use the cloze technique. For ESL students I recommend the synonym cloze. It provides a synonym as a clue and in this way becomes easier for the students to come up with the correct word and, at the same time, increases the students' vocabulary. Figure 9.3 is an example of the synonym cloze.

Figure 9.3

Seeds

Hilda planted seeds of squash in a pot of soil. Hilda put the pot near the window to <u>obtain</u> light. Without heat from the sun, plants
                 (get)
will not <u>grow.</u> The seeds developed <u>quickly.</u> The stems and leaves
  (develop)   (fast)
are green and <u>strong.</u> Weeks later the plant started having buds. The
         (healthy)
buds later <u>bloomed</u> into bright yellow flowers. A week later <u>little</u>
     (blossomed)   (small)
fruits started to grow from where the flowers grew.

The use of cloze for vocabulary development can be modified in many ways, such as: (a) providing students other passages of texts to be clozed without providing the synonyms and (b) having the students create their own cloze passages.

Semantic Mapping

Semantic maps encourage language learners to think about what they already know, and the process serves to build on and extend their knowledge. It also helps learners to see the relationship among ideas of particular topics by categorizing and connecting words. For example, on the board or a large sheet of chart paper the teacher begins listening to learners' ideas about a particular topic. Then the discussion about the words and their categories is put in writing to give students opportunities to verbalize and express ideas in the second language. Figure 9.4 illustrates the type of semantic map that can be developed.

Figure 9.4. A Semantic Map on "Food"

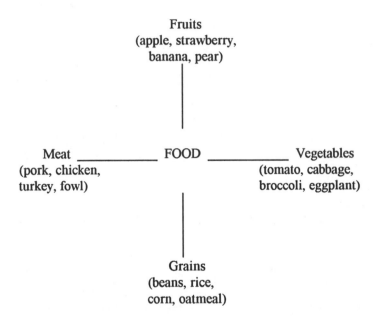

Story Mapping

This activity is useful for adolescents and adult ESL learners. It supposes that reading stories, especially short stories, dramas, and novels have structural elements that appear in many stories at all levels (setting, plot, initial event, climax). Using a "story map" assumes that the instructional model puts learners through steps of the reading process in activities that replicate in one way or another the actual mental processes learners go through in reading a text. Figure 9.5 is an example of the many variations of this model.

Figure 9.5. Story Map

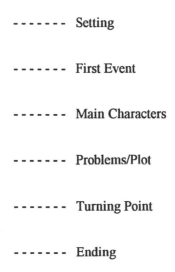

------- Setting

------- First Event

------- Main Characters

------- Problems/Plot

------- Turning Point

------- Ending

Story mapping has several functions in the ESL classroom. It can be used as: (a) a framework for designing questions to be used in teaching a story, (b) a study guide for developing routines for learners' own creative stories, (c) a summary activity, and (d) providing the framework for students' creation of their own stories.

Summary Guide

The teacher provides a brief summary of the key ideas in the text to be read during the prereading phase. This summary may be an outline, a set of key ideas, or a written paragraph. Students use the summary as a guide during their reading. Usually students summarize the text in their own words with the help of other learners and the teacher.

Book Publishing

Writing and publishing a book is a great experience for ESL students at all levels. It gives them a sense of permanence and value. It includes the planning of the topic and deciding what to say, the organization and format, as well as the shape (covers, paper, illustrations). In the process of the preparation they are continually using oral language, they write, and read. Learners are encouraged to use a variety of writing modes (expository, narrative) as well as the writing of all aspects of the book including dedications and title page. In the process, they read other books to expand their own ideas to include in the book. Having opportunities to write such author "blurbs" about themselves frequently serves as a motivation for some reluctant writers.

References

Bissex, G. L. (1980). *Gnys at wrk: A child learns to read and write.* Cambridge, MA: Harvard University Press.

Bloom, B. S. (1954). *Taxonomy of educational objectives. Handbook I. Cognitive Domain.* New York: Longman.

Clark, H. & Clark, E. (1977). *Psychology and language.* Orlando, FL: Harcourt, Brace, Jovanovich.

Dickinson, D. (1987). Oral language, literacy skills, and response to literature. In J. Squire (Ed.), *The dynamics of language learning* (pp. 184-188). Urbana: ERIC & National Conference on Research in English.

Donaldson, M. (1978). *Children's minds.* New York: W. W. Norton.

Estes, T., Gutman, D. & Harrison, E. (1988). Cultural literacy: What every educator needs to know. *Educational Leadership, 46*(1), 14-20.

Goodman, K. S., Goodman, Y. M. & Hood, W. J (1989). Developing literacy: Whole language the whole way. The whole language evaluation book. Portsmouth, NH: Heinemann, 43-54.

Hansen-Strain, L. (1987). Cognitive style and first language background in second language test performance. *TESOL*

Quarterly, 21, 565-569.

Hirsch, E. (1987). *Cultural literacy: What every American needs to know.* Boston, MA: Houghton Mifflin.

Mayher, J. S. (1990). *Uncommon sense.* Portsmouth, NH: Heinemann.

Morrow, L. (1993). Promoting voluntary interest in literature: A program that works. In A. Carrasquillo and C. Hedley (Eds.), *Whole language and the bilingual learner.* Norwood, NJ: Ablex.

Resnick, L. (1986). *Cognition and instruction: Recent theories of human competence and how it is acquired.* Psychology and learning, 4, 123-187.

Royer, J. M. & Marlo, M. S. (1991). Transfer of comprehension skills from native to second language. *Journal of Reading, 34,* 450-455.

Smith, F. (1972). *Understanding reading.* New York: Holt, Rhinehart and Winston.

Smith, F. (1990). *To think.* New York: Teachers College Press.

Stevens, R. & Slavin, R. (1991). *A cooperative learning approach to accommodating student diversity in reading and writing: Effects on handicapped and nonhandicapped students.* Baltimore, MD: Johns Hopkins University Press.

Strickland, D. & Morrow, M. (1988). Reading, writing and oral language. *The Reading Teacher, 42,* 240-41.

Verhoeven, L. T. (1987). Literacy in a second language context: Teaching immigrant children to read. *Educational review, 39,* pp. 245-259.

Weaver, C. (1988). *Reading process and practice: From socio-psycholinguistics to whole language.* Portsmouth, NH: Heinemann.

Wells, G. (1986).   *The meaning makers.*   Portsmouth, NH: Heinemann.

Wells, G. (1990).   The conditions that encourage literate thinking. *Educational Leadership, 47,* 13-17.

Wetts, G. (1987).   Apprenticeship in literacy. *Intercharge,* 1-2; 109-123.

Williams, J. D. & Capizzi-Snipper, G. (1990).   *Literacy and bilingualism.* New York: Longman.

Wyner, N. B. (1989).   Educating linguistic minorities: Public education in search for unity. *Educational Horizons, 67*(4), 173-176.

CHAPTER 10

Teaching ESL in Special Education Classrooms

In recent years the large influx of non-English or limited English speaking students in the United States has had a tremendous impact on the school system and the different communities throughout the United States. The main concern has been on how to provide appropriate education to meet the special educational needs of handicapped limited English proficient students. The recognition that these students from diverse cultural and linguistic backgrounds have special needs which require special educational interventions, specifically designed to meet their special or exceptional needs, has not come easily to the academic and social institutions in America. It has been a gradual process that has had fruition in the change and reinterpretation of laws, both at the national and state levels. Provisions of PL 94-142, which provide for the education of all handicapped children in the least restrictive environment, along with other court decisions, have contributed in addressing some of the needs of handicapped limited English proficient students. Public Law 94-142, the Education for All Handicapped Children Act (1975), is recognized by educators as the most explicit and comprehensive legislative statute in favor of the educational rights of the handicapped. The provisions of PL 94-142 take into account all the factors affecting the educational equity of handicapped children: their assessment and placement, their instruction, their parents' instructional involvement, their school environment, and other related services. As the result of this law, second language special education programs have been also recommended to meet the need to provide appropriate instruction for students whose mother-tongue is other than English, in the least restrictive environment through special educational intervention programs.

The trends in special education as they relate to LEP students reflect the relatively new field of bilingual special education (Baca & Amato, 1989; Carrasquillo, 1990), the external pressures in the form of mandated statutes at the local and federal levels, and the perceived needs of state and city agencies in their efforts to comply with these mandates. Mandated programs which provide for the planning and implementation of programs and related services to limited English proficient learners are flexible and allow for input from the different providers who are directly or indirectly responsible for the identification, assessment, placement, and delivery of instruction and related services to English learners with special needs (Cummins, 1981, 1984; Fradd & Wilen, 1990). This chapter presents an overview of issues to address when teaching English to LEP students with special learning, psychological, or emotional needs.

Assessment Issues

It is not an easy task to identify and assess the strengths and weaknesses of limited English proficient students with special needs. However, every effort should be made to ensure against inappropriate assessment procedures and referrals of these students to special education programs based on highly questionable assessment methods and materials (Maheady, Towne, Algozzine, Mercer, & Ysseldyke, 1983; Wright & Cruz, 1983). The first step is to determine if a student's communication and learning problems are the result of an inability to perform in the English language. The second step is determining which assessment tools are adequately designed to measure children's language. The third step is identifying assessment tools that can help teachers and evaluators differentiate second language acquisition problem from a real handicap.

The most prominent component placing certain groups at a disadvantage is language. The disadvantage of language does not only mean subjecting children to be assessed in a language that is not their mother-tongue, since the language-centered problems are more intrinsic and subjected to the effects of other variables and not a simple matter of choice between languages. Different groups not only speak different languages, have different ways of expressing their view of the world and their social and psychological preferences, they have different ways for expressing meaning. They also have different ways for verbal conceptualism, feelings, and demonstrating different patterns of usage.

Limited English proficient students are over-represented in special education programs. This over-representation problem of minority groups including limited English proficient students in special education for learning disabilities has been criticized as being directly connected to test biases (Cloud, 1990; Cummins, 1984; Fradd & Wilen, 1990; Garcia & Ortiz, 1988; Wright & Cruz, 1983). Most attempts to rectify test biases have not been successful. Some critics believe that even if truly non-discriminatory assessment measures were developed, they would do little to reverse or reduce the systematic bias that has been documented to occur prior to and following assessment. Given this assessment of the problem in test bias and subsequent over-representation of minority and limited English proficient students in special education programs, many educators are carefully looking at options and alternatives for effective instruction to minority and limited English proficient students in special education programs.

The most frequent reasons for referral of limited English proficient students to special education programs for the learning disabled are problems in language and reading, which indicate that the language characteristics of learning disabled students play an important role not only in the placement of such students but also in the design of the instructional program (Carrasquillo & Reyes-Bonilla, 1990). LEP special education students are identified as LEP by some type of language proficiency assessment procedure, and they are identified as handicapped by a multidisciplinary assessment process. However, Cummins (1984) emphasized that the type of proficiency required in most tests can take up to seven years to be realized by second language learners, and in many cases students have not spent enough time in second language programs, thus affecting test outcomes. He described general characteristics of these students related to their areas of handicap and discussed recommended instructional strategies. In this chapter we are assuming that those LEP students in special education classrooms are handicapped at some level of the neurological, cognitive, or emotional level. It is also assumed that the students' native language was used in assessing their handicap, that students have been identified as having limited English proficiency and a particular handicapping condition, and that long and short term goals were written in the individualized educational plan (IEP) based on the needs of the students and the particular special education curriculum, including ESL instruction. The short term goals are formulated and based on an in-depth analysis of the special education (including ESL) teaching strategies and suggested instructional materials. This assessment helps educators to understand students' current stage of English language acquisition; their strengths and weaknesses in particular skill areas (listening, speaking, reading, and writing); their emotional and motivational status; their language learning styles; personality characteristics; their interests and needs; and the amount of opportunities (formal and informal) they will have to engage in the acquisition of English (Cloud, 1990).

Learning Disabled LEP Students

Learning disabilities are one of the areas with more representation of LEP students. Jacobs (1983) defined learning disabilities as a group of disorders interfering with the development and/or use of abilities in listening, speaking, reading, writing, reasoning, and mathematics. The cause is often unknown; the disorders are caused neither by other handicapped conditions (emotional disturbance, visual or hearing impairment or mental retardation) nor by environmental deprivation. Research studies on the language characteristics of learning disabled children indicate that these students show deficits in areas such as syntax, semantics, and communicative competence (Bryan & Bryan, 1986; Bryan, Donahue & Pearl, 1981; Carrasquillo & Reyes-Bonilla, 1990; Feagans, 1983; Jacobs, 1983). In the area of syntax (the arrangement of words into meaningful phrases/sentences and the means by which such relationships are shown), the literature shows that these children with learning disabilities are less capable than most children in detecting semantic structures, and they demonstrate significant delays in the acquisition of syntax. If students have difficulty in the acquisition or use of syntactic rules, it is likely that oral language development will be disorganized and difficult to understand. Idol-Maestes (1980) and Vogel (1977) have identified common syntactical difficulties among learning-disabled children.

These are: (a) determining if a sentence is a statement of information or a question, (b) filling in deleted words in spoken paragraphs, (c) completing morphological tests and exercises, (d) oral retailing of or restating of information, (e) repeating sentences, (f) appropriate use of verb-tense markers (whether the action is present, past, or future), and (g) incorrect use of past tense responses. Hence, limited facility with syntax appears to depress the learning disabled students' performances in reading and listening to academic materials. It has also been found that such children's syntax use in speech was less complex than that employed by their non-disabled peers, and even if the syntax was correct and complex, it was found to be limited (Bryan & Bryan, 1986).

Learning-disabled children are often found deficient in semantics (the understanding and production of words) when compared with "normal" children of the same age. Pearl, Donahue & Ryan (1981) have identified specific language deficits in: (a) expressive language, (b) language comprehension, (c) generating or recalling stories, (d) naming verbal opposites, (e) defining words, (f) retrieving words from memory, (g) responding with words, and (h) formulating sentences.

Recent research on the area of communicative competence indicates that learning disabled children are less likely than their normal peers to make speech changes, depending on the audience (Bryan, Donahue & Pearl, 1981; Perlmutter & Ryan, 1984). These children lack the pragmatic skills of asking questions, persuading, responding to messages, and supporting an argument. Also, these children have difficulties in constructing messages that allow listeners to make correct interpretations (Bryan & Bryan, 1986; Bryan, Donahue & Pearl, 1981). Many of these children have difficulties in eliciting positive responses from others and are less skillful than developmentally normal achievers in using language in a variety of social contexts.

All of the above general learning characteristics of learning disabled students need to be assessed through the learners' first language. Limited English disabled students show some of the above characteristics. In addition, they are not proficient in the language of the school. Therefore, special education programs need to provide them with the appropriate instructional environment and adequate ESL programs.

Mentally Retarded LEP Students

There is a significant group of LEP students enrolled in classrooms for the mentally retarded. Low performance on academic tasks on a continuous basis is usually what motivates schools to recommend students for evaluation. In many instances, a significant percentage of these students do not belong in special education classrooms because their low performances are due to lack of English skills as well as lack of school experiences. It is said that these students are misplaced in special education classrooms. This section addresses the other group–a smaller group of LEP students who due to other factors (such as incidence of malnutrition, drugs, poor pre- or post-natal care) have been improperly diagnosed and placed in classrooms for the mentally retarded.

Mental retardation has been defined as a significant sub-average general intellectual functioning existing concurrently with deficits in adaptive behavior that manifests during the developmental period. This population is usually divided into the mildly, moderately trainable or educable, and the severely retarded. While both groups require modified instructional settings, severely retarded students are placed in highly specialized learning environments. Characteristics of the moderately and mildly retarded include: (a) difficulty in generalizing and understanding abstracts, (b) overall academic retardation–significantly below grade level in all subjects, (c) immaturity evidenced in play and other interests both in and out of school, (d) sensory and coordination problems, (e) easily frustrated, (f) vocabulary of a much younger child, (g) slower growth and development patterns, and (h) poor self-help skills.

LEP retarded students need a very carefully sequenced instructional curriculum. In order to plan for the introduction of English, educators need to look at learners' language development in the first language, level of socialization in both cultures–primary and English–emotional maturity, academic achievement, as well as intelligence. English as a second language instruction needs to emphasize functional skills necessary for survival and community living, the enhancement of memory, as well as generalizations from experience. The attitude of the ESL program should be that these students are capable of learning when provided with a carefully individualized sequence of instruction at a level of students' cognitive and linguistic growth.

Emotionally Disabled LEP Students

Within the educational setting, emotionally disabled students are those whose behaviors may be discordant in their relationship with others, and/or whose academic achievement may be impaired due to the inability to learn. These students' current behavior manifests either in an extreme or a persistent failure to adapt and function intellectually, emotionally, and socially at a level commensurate with their chronological age (De Blassie, 1983). Characteristics of emotional disabilities include: (a) depression, hypochondria, regression (such as thumb sucking), (b) overly dependent behavior, (c) compulsive behaviors, (d) being accident prone (enjoying attention), (e) feelings and moods that are out of proportion, (f) conversation with self or imaginary figures, (g) extreme anxiety, (h) refusal to verbalize, (i) strong uncontrollable fears or frequent crying, (j) seeming distracted or extremely withdrawn, and (k) aggressive behavior. In order to assess an emotionally disabled child or individual, several of the above characteristics need to be manifested and need to impede learning. Educators need to be clear that LEP students may reflect these characteristics due to social and temporal changes such as assimilation or acculturation, or mainly as a normal reaction to a new culture and a new language. These behaviors are expected to diminish once students adapt to a bilingual and bicultural environment.

ESL instruction must be carefully tailored so as not to increase students' emotional disability. ESL teachers need to show care and concern for LEP students' language and academic growth. It is important that teachers use the English language to show positive reinforcement of the children's successes. Appropriate behaviors should be accompanied with a friendly and encouraging attitude. Through ESL tasks that contain a variety of linguistic activities that are both interesting and culturally relevant, students will be maintained on task in an environment conducive to learning.

Language Disordered LEP Students

Language disorders may be defined as difficulties in the manipulation of propositional meanings which are likely to interfere with mental growth and development. Some conditions associated with language disorders include organic, psychological, environmental, and functional factors. Damage to the central nervous system can affect language processing and movements of the musculature involved in speech production. Also, hearing loss can affect language acquisition. Psychological disabilities can be associated with speech and language disorders. These psychological disabilities may not allow children to use elements (spatial and time concepts, for example) to process language or to engage in communicative tasks. These language disorders can, in turn, be the cause of other conditions. For example, stutterers could develop emotional disorders due to the inability to produce language verbally. Disorders of speech may affect the acquisition of a second language. In a "disordered speech" the production follows social rules and the deviance of these social rules affect the exchange of messages between members of the community (Perkins, 1977). A language disorder exists when individuals' comprehension and/or expression does not compare favorably with the language used by their peers (Linares, 1983). The language disordered child may present moderate to severe difficulties in one or more aspects of the language, that being in the lexicon, the semantics, the phonology, and the syntax.

It is assumed that the students' native language was used in assessing their language disorders. This assessment includes students' hearing, language comprehension, as well as speech production, and pragmatic use of the students' native language. Limited English proficient language disordered students need therapeutic intervention, in which language pathologists help students in their native language to be better language receivers and communicators. Language therapists help individuals in using the primary language to communicate using rules for voice, fluency, articulation production, and language comprehension and production (Linares, 1983). ESL instruction for this group needs to be carefully planned as not to interfere with the intervention in the primary language. English as a second language instruction should be taught informally using functional tasks in which students are involved in interactive communicative activities of interest to them. ESL instruction should not be rushed. It needs to be gradually introduced providing comfortable English language classroom environments for LEP students.

Recommended ESL Strategies

English as a second language instruction has been succinctly defined as a structured language acquisition program designed to teach English to students whose native language is not English. English as a second language in special education requires special second language strategies. It is an individualized instructional program in which the ESL goal, objectives, methods, and materials are individualized as part of the student's comprehensive individualized educational program. It is a program in which knowledge of the disability is required to plan effective programs (Ortiz, 1984). For example, in planning an ESL program for LEP students with emotional disorders, knowledge of the educational, emotional, and physical needs of the students are integrated with adequate second language teaching strategies in order for the ESL program to be effective for that particular population. Current practices of teaching a second language indicates that:

1. Children will participate in cognitive and linguistic tasks as long as these tasks are interesting and relate to the children's own interests (Krashen & Terrell, 1984; Ortiz, 1984). Children must be active learners. Language skills are emphasized as part of the job that has to be done in which there are instrumental/practical values for listening, speaking, reading, and writing in the second language. Children have a need to understand concepts through active and motivated learning. The teacher's role is to help students learn and verbalize concepts, not to correct their grammar or punctuation. In special education classrooms, motivating and creative activities play a key role in how much cognitive involvement students put into what they do. Second language activity tasks need to maintain students' interest from

the beginning to the end, and if the teacher recognizes that students are losing interest, then that is the time to move them into another learning task.

2. For language-disabled students language instruction should not be broken down into parts (phonic or grammar rules), but into meaningful tasks. The instructional focus of the task should be on the message (communication and understanding), not on the form. Language is a natural creative process rather than one of habit formation. Teachers should provide guidance and practice in thinking in the language rather than mere repetitive drills (Carrasquillo & Reyes-Bonilla, 1990). Cummins (1984) suggests a second language program which is embedded in a meaningful concrete context and supported by a wide range of paralinguistic cues which allows students to infer the intended meaning and simultaneously acquire the second language. Second language learning must occur as part of meaningful communication, making language learning more enjoyable for students since they will focus on language as a means of accomplishing a cognitive activity. Students need to see the second language classroom as one where they go to acquire knowledge about the world as well as about the language being learned. Every activity in the classroom has a cognitive and linguistic purpose from lining up in the yard (learning about structure and organization) to discussing the lunchroom menu of the day (learning about what is considered a balanced diet).

3. Providing for diversity of classroom interaction enables students to participate in cognitively challenging activities (Ortiz, 1984). For example, in any given time period, opportunities need to be provided for whole class instruction, cooperative or collaborative learning, small group interactions, and one-to-one interaction. Language students can benefit from whole class instruction at the initial stage when they are just beginning to get acquainted with the language and they are going through the silent period (Krashen & Terrell, 1984). Choral activities and pattern drills may also be used. A whole class format is of vital importance: students work in small groups, encouraging them to listen, speak, read, and write in the second language. Children need various opportunities for sustained one-to-one interaction, which involves an almost equal number of turns attuned to the children's

language development. One-to-one situations are more conducive to encouraging attempts at talking.

4. In some situations the language of the classroom may need to be simplified to be meaningful and comprehensible. In other words, students must be able to understand its content although they might not understand every word included in the sentence (Carrasquillo & Reyes-Bonilla, 1990; Cloud, 1990; Cummins, 1981; 1984). For this reason, the language being used needs to be simple and understandable. This does not mean that the teacher has to change the tone of voice or speed in posing a sentence, thinking that this oral approach will provide for greater student understanding. However, the teacher needs to understand that these second language learners have a limited vocabulary and limited syntactical and grammatical structure. At the beginning, sentences need to be syntactically and grammatically simple and short. One way of simplifying language is through the simplification of the vocabulary. The amount of new vocabulary or phrases should be limited to the level of student understanding. Also, knowing isolated words without a context has little meaning to the students. This by no means suggests that vocabulary will be kept to a minimum. It means that new words will be used in meaningful contexts. Vocabulary will be emphasized through the use of content and usage, repetition and expansion. Vocabulary should be selected for immediate need or usefulness (family, home, TV programs) and should be within the students' experience.

5. Syntax and grammar should be presented in small structured units, systematically progressing from concepts that have been learned, moving up to the next level of difficulty. The teacher can relate previously learned knowledge and skills to new tasks; simplifying to a certain extent the mechanical aspects of the language, and facilitating communication through non-verbal gestures and body language, and relying on motor activities.

6. Classroom instructional activities should integrate the four areas of listening, speaking, reading, and writing. There was a popular misconception in English as a second language that oral skills must be mastered before written skills. But in the last decade, the focus has been on the integration of skills in which learners engage in developing language, reading, and writing skills. It is

not necessary for English learners to achieve complete fluency in the spoken language before moving to written language (Krashen & Terrell, 1984). Listening and reading are receptive skills, which always exceed the productive skills of speaking and writing. Language proficiency is balanced between the two productive processes of speaking and writing. Students can comprehend through listening and reading and can communicate through speaking and writing tasks. From the beginning, students learn to use language in meaningful contexts as part of an attempt to understand and relate to the world around them. Language is a process of thought and production that must be used by second language learners if both processes are to be mastered. The integration of language in classroom activities includes auditory processing, oral language development, reading-related activities, and creative writing. Children can comprehend a great deal more (through listening and reading) than they demonstrate in speaking and writing tasks.

7. Instruction should provide for the development of reading skills. When students are reading in a second language, they need to fully utilize their experiences and knowledge to acquire immediate comprehension. There will be times when students, due to their own cultural and linguistic backgrounds, have little or no background on a given topic. Activities to generate background knowledge need to be provided in the classroom and need to be of a more concrete nature. These activities may include viewing of a film, working with concrete objects, prior reading, or discussion on the topics through books, newspapers, pictures, or any other concrete material. In order to help students develop reading skills in English, the following strategies are recommended: (a) continually reinforce the development of the oral language, (b) expand student's vocabulary, (c) use strategies that involve figuring out word or phrase meanings, and (d) expose students to a variety of reading selections.

8. The provision for communicative writing is necessary. Writing is viewed as a creative medium of communication. It is a difficult and abstract form of verbal thinking. Creative as well as practical writing needs to be functional and requires creativity and knowledge of writing skills. Students react differently to assigned writing tasks because of differences in developmental

stages, home classroom environments, and their interests. Writing, as well as speaking, is almost always directed towards an audience whose expectations shape the form and content of the message. Students need to listen to stories as well as create their own. Experience, getting in touch with one's feelings, and having many opportunities to write are necessary ingredients of writing. Students need a rich and varied literacy environment to which they can add their first-hand knowledge and experiences and communicate using the second language.

9. English as a second language programs should provide for a variety of language instructional techniques. The field of English as a second language has been enriched by literature of successful language methodologies. It is recommended that a variety of strategies be used, such as problem solving, role playing, total physical response, story telling, experience charts, dialogues, content-based language emphasis, semantic mapping (especially for the development of vocabulary), language experience approach, and natural and communicative approaches for oral communication. These approaches have been described in other chapters of this book, especially in chapters 7, 8, and 9. The following strategies have been found to be very useful in special education classrooms.

Role Playing. The role playing technique creates a dramatic situation in the classroom, in part by simply acting out dialogues in the teaching setting. The interest is in oral material which synthesizes useful vocabulary, realistic context, and social and psycholinguistic features. Role playing releases inhibitions and in doing so, encourages humor. It allows students to express themselves while it exposes them to English and the American culture.

Problem Solving. Through problem solving students work on topics which are important to them. Students are given the mechanism to share facts and information with the class in small or large group settings using oral and written language. Again students are using the language for a cognitive task. They feel free enough to use English to express themselves without seriously thinking that they are making mistakes in the second language.

Content-Based Language Tasks. The literature is prolific on how the language classroom can use content in the ESL classroom. There exists a long list of activities in which language is used to fulfill communicative purposes. The following are some of these activities: (a) to seek information on a given topic (e.g., Earth's gravity), (b) to give information in a specific area (e.g., fertilization of plants), (c) to express reaction to a particular topic (e.g., to a TV program, to a movie, to a controversial issue, such as the Persian Gulf War), (d) to solve a problem (e.g., the need to provide solar energy to plants), and (e) to display one's achievement (e.g., demonstrating computer literacy).

Total Physical Response. This is a good strategy in the early stages of second language learning. The teacher gives a command and models the physical movement to carry out the command. At first, students focus only on listening comprehension by responding to the commands with the appropriate physical movement. In the production stage they begin speaking, and eventually move to reading and writing.

Natural Approach Techniques. These strategies focus on providing a context in the classroom for natural language acquisition to occur, with acquirers receiving maximum comprehension input while providing opportunities in the classroom to feel less anxious toward the second language. Language content is: (a) based on the student's interests, (b) absence of initial correction, (c) avoidance of initial production, and (e) acceptance of the native language for communicative purposes. The students' native language and activities focusing on non-verbal and auditory processing are used in the pre-production stage to facilitate students' comprehension and ease of the target language.

Semantic Mapping. Research in vocabulary development indicates that the larger the number of words that language learners have, the better their auditory and written comprehension. Word meaning is not acquired in isolation but within a conceptual framework. Vocabulary acquisition is an interactive process that focuses on the contributions of the learners' prior knowledge of the new concept. Semantic mapping is a strategy of structuring information in graphic form by displaying related words in categories. Although this is a strategy recommended for a pre-reading activity, it has its place in oral development too, in which case the teacher may show pictures with the words in the graphic form.

Effective schools and educational systems must plan for appropriate special education for language minority students with special needs. The students who have been identified as limited English proficient with special needs should receive specialized instructional services that account for their linguistic and cultural characteristics as well as their identified disabilities.

References

Baca, L. & Amato, C. (1989). Bilingual special education: Training Issues. *Exceptional Children, 56*, 168-173.

Bryan, T. H. & Bryan, J. H. (1986). *Understanding learning disabilities.* Palo Alto, CA: Mayfield.

Bryan, T., Donahue, M. & Pearl, R. (1981). Learning disabled children's communicative competence on referential communication tasks. *Journal of Pediatric Psychology, 6*, 383-393.

Carrasquillo, A. & Reyes-Bonilla, R. M. (1990) Teaching a second language to limited English proficient learning-disabled students. In A. L. Carrasquillo & R. Baecher (Eds.), *Teaching the bilingual special education student* (pp. 67-89). Norwood, NJ: Ablex.

Carrasquillo, A. (1990). Bilingual special education: The important connection. In A. Carrasquillo & R. Baecher (Eds.), *Teaching the bilingual special education student* (pp. 4-24). Norwood, NJ: Ablex.

Cloud, N. (1990). Planning and implementing an English as a second language program. In A. L. Carrasquillo & R. Baecher (Eds.), *Teaching the bilingual special education student* (pp. 106-131). Norwood, NJ: Ablex.

Cummins, J. (1981). Bilingualism and special education: Program and pedagogical issues. *Learning Disability Quarterly, 6*, 373-386.

Cummins, J. (1984). Bilingualism and special education: *Issues in assessment and pedagogy.* San Diego, CA: College Hill Press.

De Blassie, R. P. (1983). Emotional and behavioral disorders in bilingual children. In D. R. Omark & J. G. Erickson (Eds.), *The bilingual exceptional child* (pp. 55-68). San Diego, CA: College Hill Press.

Feagans, L. (1983). Discourse processes in learning disabled children. In J. D. McKinney & L. Feagans (Eds.), *Current topics in learning disabilities* (Vol. 1, pp. 87-115). Norwood, NJ: Ablex.

Fradd, S. H. & Wilen, D. K (1990). *Using interpreters and translators to meet the needs of handicapped families.* Program Information Guide Series. Washington, DC: National Clearinghouse for Bilingual Education.

Garcia, S. B. & Ortiz, A. A. (June, 1988). Preventing inappropriate referrals of language minority students to special education. *FOCUS* (No. 5). Rosslyn, VA: National Clearinghouse for Bilingual Education.

Idol-Maestes, L. (1980). Auditory perceptual ability of normal children aged five through eight. *Journal of Genetic Psychology, 3,* 289-294.

Jacobs, L. (1983). Cognition and learning disabilities. *Teaching Exceptional Children, 16,* 213-217.

Krashen, S. & Terrell, T. D. (1984). *The natural approach: Language acquisition in the classroom.* London: Pergamon.

Linares, N. (1983). Management of communicatively handicapped Hispanic American children. In D. R. Omark & J. G. Erickson (Eds.), *The bilingual exceptional child* (pp. 145-162). San Diego, CA: College Hill Press.

Maheady, L., Towne, R., Algozzine, B., Mercer, J. & Ysseldyke, J. (1983). Minority overrepresentation: A case for alternative practice prior to referral. *Learning Disability Quarterly, 6,* 448-455.

Ortiz, A. A. (1984). Choosing the language of instruction of exceptional bilingual children. *Teaching Exceptional Children, 16,* 208-212.

Pearl, R., Donahue, M. & Ryan, T. (1981). Children's responses to non-explicit requests for clarification. *Perceptual and Motor Skills, 53,* 919-925.

Perkins, W. (1977). *Speech pathology: An applied behavioral science.* St. Louis: C. V. Mosby.

Perlmutter, B. & Ryan, J. (1984). First impressions, ingratiation, and the learning disabled child. *Journal of Learning Disabilities, 3,* 157-161.

United States Department of Education. (1975). *Education of the Handicapped Act.* Washington, DC: Government Printing Office.

Vogel, S. A. (1977). Morphological ability in normal and dyslexic children. *Journal of Learning Disabilities, 7,* 103-109.

Wright, P. & Cruz, R. S. (1983). Ethnic composition of special education programs in California. *Learning Disability Quarterly, 6,* 379-385.

CHAPTER 11

The Human Factor: Teachers, Administration, and Parents

The academic, social, and mental development of learners has been the overriding objective of education throughout the history of instruction and learning. One key characteristic of the qualitative differences between the most successful schools is the human connection. The administrator, the teacher, and parents are the most influential human components in determining the success or failure of the teaching-learning process. The attention given to these human components is of great importance to all areas of the school education but more so to the field of English as a second language. In ESL human relationships play a vital role in identifying classrooms and schools. It is only in contemporary times that teaching, administering, and parenting have been examined and evaluated in terms of their content and quality of human skills. Human factors which are embodied in the ESL teacher, the principal, and the parents, all participating in the school's effort with goals and objectives moving in the same direction, are essential elements in providing LEP students with the high quality ESL instruction and general education they are entitled to. In this context the teaching of ESL must go beyond the intellectual and the cognitive to give emphasis to the use of second language for the affective and human purposes of life. English as a second language instruction should provide for autonomous interaction in which the affective elements of human relationships are given priority. In this way, mastery of the second language contributes to develop respect and understanding for each other, celebrate differences, and share commonalties. This chapter provides a brief overview of some of those human skills of teaching, administering,

187

and parenting that play an important and positive role in the education of limited English proficient students.

The Parent Factor

Who are the parents of ESL students? The question may be answered by analyzing the types of students who are enrolled in ESL programs:

1. A significant number are new arrivals coming from immigrant parents, who came to the United States primarily for economic, political, religious, or family reasons.
2. Other students were born in the United States but come from a non-English-speaking home. Many Puerto Rican, Dominican, and Cuban children are good examples of LEP students with long residence in the United States.
3. A smaller group of LEP children are those whose parents are temporarily living in the United States for job related purposes. A significant group of Japanese students falls into this category.

The above characteristics indicate that parents of LEP children have different ethnic, linguistic, and socioeconomic characteristics. In addition, their social, financial, and legal status in the United States contribute in many ways to shape, along with the school, the character, linguistic, and academic personality of their children. Knowledge about the status of the parents in the United States and their relationship with their children help schools to understand better parents' aspirations for their children as well as their limitations. Parents of LEP children need to be able to feel at ease with the school that their children attend so that they can help their children to succeed in school. However, schools also need to understand parents' cultural linguistic background and their daily struggles and their educational strategies in helping their children. The following paragraphs describe parents of LEP students, their diversity as well as their educational role.

Immigrant parents represent a new challenge to the educational establishment (Fass, 1989). Although early immigrants to this country were for the most part English-speaking, and the transition was nominal, non-institutional aspects of education, such as apprenticeships, self-study, and ethnic mutual aid societies, were responsible for much of the adjustment to the new way of life. Today immigrant parents depend heavily on public institutions to educate their children. The private tutoring, charity schools, proprietary schools, the apprenticeship system, and education provided by religious denominations' service are not available to these parents. Most immigrant parents place great importance on the role of school for their children. They want them to do well. Most parents are supportive of the school's mission; what most of them are not aware of is that they need to be active partners of their children's educational success. But even if they are aware, their daily struggles do not permit them to be more actively involved. For example, a significant group of LEP students and parents are illegal immigrants. Living in a state of anxiety, they secure employment wherever they can find it, most frequently receiving pay below poverty wages. They suffer abuses of employers who have them at their mercy. These parents are burdened with the constant uncertainty of job security and economic solvency. At times, they work double shifts or more than one job to make ends meet. In this context, they may not be as alert as they should be to look after the best interests of their children at school.

A significant group of parents of LEP children come from lower socioeconomic classes (Knap, Trunbull & Shields, 1990). They experience most of the problems associated with poverty, unemployment, poor health care and housing, crime, and other societal ills. Parents in low socioeconomic classes are always striving for better living conditions. Mobility is a function of such striving. School authorities are very concerned about the effects of mobility on student progress. Public school records reveal a high number of moves by students in elementary grades as early as kindergarten. The payoff for moving usually is the promise of increased living space, privacy, and in many instances, an escape from areas of overt crime and drug activity. Mobility and human relationships within the family settings are conditioned by living space needs. Apartments occupied by immigrant families often are subdivisions of larger apartments. Where an indigenous family of four may vacate a large apartment, two immigrant families may move in. In many cases, the main family may rent rooms to couples or single occupants. It is not unusual in inner city areas to find large families of six or seven in a one-bedroom apartment. In such crowded situations, families must interact and communicate in ways that are sometimes detrimental to the individuals in the setting, especially to the children. Privacy, which is essential in developing a sense of personal identity, especially during teenage years, is very important to the child. Because of the large numbers, many neighborhoods are considered immigrant islands where parents develop close-knit associations. Much of the emerging multicultural character of the schools is due to the presence of parents and their influence on the school culture. In many areas, there are schools and other institutions where the immigrant language is used as much as the second language. In these schools, often bilingual schools, first and second language development is the medium through which LEP children address their educational needs and establish their identity.

Immigrant parents are especially alert when medical and health concerns about their children arise. Since they have to depend mostly on public health and medical care, they are diligent in observing school regulations concerning immunization and other requirements. They depend in great measure on private ethnic medical care centers, whose primary function is to address the needs of illegal aliens who are not entitled to medicare or other public health care services.

Limited English proficient children come from family constellations that include more siblings than the average indigenous family. Extended family members, who live in proximity with the family, often live and interact co-dependently with the core family. Many parents work and allow responsibility for the daily care of the children to grandparents or other members of the extended family. Often, they allow neighbors and acquaintances with residential proximity to care for the children during and after school. Given the preoccupation with securing basic needs of everyday life, and given the fact that most have had limited educational experiences, these parents express concern about the importance of education for their children but are not consistent in acting out their responsibilities that go with the schooling of their children. Most parents of LEP children do not have sufficient English skills to be active partners with the schools in teaching and caring for their children. Parents are faced with problems of survival from day to day, and do not seem to respond the way principals and teachers would like them to. Teachers like to teach in schools where parents participate and care for their children. They feel that the saddest part of being a teacher is seeing parents that really do not care for their children. Alienation between parents and teachers often results. One teacher, expressing his feeling of frustration, said that he never felt treated as less than an adult by his colleagues in teaching, but he did by his administrators, counselors, and much more by parents (Godar, 1990). Most of the time this pessimistic view of parents is due to sociocultural differences in family life and the ways that schools respond to these differences. This situation reflects a pattern of separation between parents and schools.

The home environment and parental attitudes become crucial in determining how well or how poorly the children will advance during their development, both in school and in the community. It is difficult for parents, who are preoccupied with their own problems, to show educational priority for their children's education and to show a healthy attachment to their children, who are apt to develop their parents' general outlook on life through daily interaction with them. Schools need to work with language minority parents to convey to them what schools in the United States want from them and from their children. At the same time that schools show parents that they recognize and appreciate their culture because it is reflected in the school's curriculum, parents need to positively be re-affirmed that they are partners in education. Ways and means need to be identified in which parents can clearly see their roles. These roles include: (a) better school norms, (b) positive attitude toward school, (c) trust in the teachers, (d) help children with their homework, (e) ensure that their children attend school regularly and on time, (f) drive for academic achievement, (g) participate in the school's academic and social functions, and (h) attend parent conferences. As attractive as these parent/school expectations may appear, such participation does not reach its full potential if parents do not share the school's decision-making process. As decision makers, parents can take the initiative if the school is not providing the quality education they expect for their children. Parents, with the guidance of the school personnel, can take an active role in maintaining home-school communication.

The nature of parental involvement in schools has gone into a transition from tacit acceptance to active participation in policy and decision making (Kantrowitz & Wingert, 1989). Reforms in the way schools plan their programs and develop goals and objectives have given parents an opportunity to play roles other than those of the traditional "coffee and cake" providers. As lay people, they may not be able to walk into a school and be principals or teachers. They are, however, equipped and entitled to be partners in the education of their children. In schools where the role of the parent is welcomed and incorporated into the fabric of the school's decision-making climate, the human relationships stand to be healthier and more favorable in providing effective educational services to all students, including second language learners. Effective parent involvement is evident when they actively participate in school-based management and shared decision-making committees. They are an essential component in school, district-wide, and city-wide committees. Many parents in districts with large immigrant and LEP populations play leading roles as members of community boards or special educational organizations.

The ESL Teacher

In today's education, the role of the ESL classroom teacher is a prominent one. ESL teachers play roles that go beyond just imparting instruction; their role must take into account human elements in their relationship with LEP students. Therefore, ESL teachers constitute a vital element in humanizing the total educational experience of LEP students in school. How can we describe this teacher? To what extent do the personality and human values entertained by ESL teachers affect their teaching performance? In the process of instruction, these teachers must be aware of the diverse ethnic and linguistic groups, personalities, and characters present among students. They must be empathetic in order to understand and be sensitive to the students' sociocultural and linguistic makeup and needs. This empathy will also help ESL teachers in developing proper teaching strategies and media techniques through which more effective instruction can occur. It is thus suggested that cultural understanding and sensitivity go hand in hand with good ESL teaching and the positive perception of what a good ESL teacher should be.

It takes people and other living things beyond artifacts to convert a house into a home. It takes good ESL teachers to induce language proficiency through ways other than pure cognitive and linguistic inputs. ESL teachers must consider the child not only as a receiver of cognitive language skills but also as a whole being with feelings, personality, prior knowledge, and other human attributes that play important roles in the acquisition of language. Second language must be functional and for immediate use. The intellectual objectives for learning a language are no longer as relevant as the functional demands of immediate use. For learning to continue in the classroom, teachers have to provide a climate that will further foster these students' natural inclinations. Rather than stressing that students discover the "correct" answer in the textbook or in the teacher's head, teachers attempt to enhance the probability of students' own "discoveries" (Lovitt, 1990). It is a common understanding that teachers are more successful when they grant the students equity and equality of opportunity. ESL teachers must go beyond general instruction to view individual differences among students as more important to the strategic teaching than their similarities. Such differences provide teachers with opportunities to differentiate instruction and fulfill more of the needs of individual students.

ESL instruction has come a long way from the rote methods of traditional education, which limited the child to interaction with the book and the teacher, to natural methods that immerse the students in all kinds of functional learning experiences. It is for this reason that ESL teachers of today should be acquainted with the culture and language of their students. A working knowledge of the language helps both teachers and children to build bridges of conceptual understanding during the process of teaching and learning.

The personality of the teacher should be inviting and non-threatening to LEP students. Most language learners become very teacher dependent during their language formative years. English as a second language teachers must have the ability to make students feel valuable, capable, and always part of the social setting. Any feeling of isolation resulting from lack of understanding of the indigenous language should be minimized. The teacher must realize that children have the same needs that adults have. In addition to the basic needs such as food, warmth, and shelter, and in addition to the need for safety and security, students need to belong, to be loved, to be respected, and to sustain high self-esteem (Eisner, 1991; Pai, 1990). These needs are important for both the teacher and the student.

ESL teachers need to be energetic, creative, self-motivating, spontaneous, efficient, and tolerant. In working with children, the ESL teacher should always act on a foundation of human values. In class, effective ESL teachers create classroom conditions which enable the second language learners to work towards satisfying their basic needs. It is important that the teaching process is of such quality as to inhibit feelings of alienation and boredom. The tendency to limit the language learning experience to the confines of the classroom should be resisted. When this is not possible, ESL teachers must be able to create a classroom atmosphere where children can actively engage in linguistic activities that are diverse and appealing. There is not much ESL teachers can do about the physical structure of the classroom, but the classroom environment can be made comfortable, informal, and visually interesting. The teacher can change the climate by altering traditional seating patterns to make students be more receptive to interacting.

English as a second language teachers must have the ability to set the conditions in which language development can occur in an atmosphere of creativity; where children are open to experiences and perceptions without being confined to rigid categories of learning. From early stages, ESL teachers should work out teaching strategies where students are on their own, trying to use the second language for normal purposes such as establishing social relations; seeking and giving information; expressing reactions; learning or teaching others to do something; hiding intentions; talking their way out of trouble; persuading, discouraging, entertaining others; sharing leisure activities; displaying their achievements; acting out social roles; discussing ideas, and playing with language for the fun of it. Teachers need to show the ability to make the teaching experience of value for the moment, without regard for future consequences. Children learn best when each activity points to the possibility of another and new experience, and to the shaping of ideas in which the language can be manipulated and used in new and significant ways (Postman, 1979). When the ESL teacher takes delight in novelty and ambiguity, even in absurdity, in order to foster an atmosphere of joy and play, and when the teacher helps the student to be strong enough to rely on his or her own internal evaluation, this teacher is creative and most effective. English as a second language teachers must have the ability to induce in the students self-evaluation and self-criticism as a condition for self-respect and self-expression (Hawley & Hawley, 1975; Knap, Trunbull & Shields, 1990).

The relationship between teacher and principal makes a great deal of difference in the quality of services to the student. Godar (1990) interviewed a teacher for an opinion on her principal. Her reply was: "The principal we have now is here for the children first . . . even if that's at the expense of the teacher, and that's the way it should be. But she is very concerned about my concerns about my teaching, because I think every teacher has a different style, and different things that make it work for him or her. She tries to get to know that, and offers you support that you need." Good feelings and respect for the principal as an instructional leader are essential if the teacher is to be humanistic and productive.

The Principal As an Instructional Leader

Principals of today's schools are under a great deal of pressure to demonstrate leadership in academic achievement. The pressures on them are primarily expressed through the ranking of their schools from excellent to poor, according to the results of citywide standardized reading and mathematics tests given each year to their students. Even principals themselves have come to accept such rankings as a standard evaluation of their schools. Also, there is a generation of principals and other high level instructional administrators in the public school system whose training and performance characteristics reflect only cognitive, conceptual, and management skills (Bowles, 1968; Pai, 1990). Until recently, qualifying tests for principals and administrators evaluated proficiency in only those three areas of instructional leadership. As a result, the knowledge, abilities, and skills brought into the school by such administrative leaders seldom complement another set of very important skills–human skills.

As an instructional leader, the principal must be aware of the importance of human factors in the classroom and must also recognize the importance of multicultural education (including language) and values in education (Hawley & Hawley, 1975; Klopf, 1979). Principals should be keenly aware of the strengths of the school's students, especially as they relate to general learning, personality, culture, and language. In their organizational scheme, they should be capable of giving priority to those activities which maximize language learning through multicultural and multilingual interaction with peers and adults. In urban schools, when faced with budget crises, principals have a tendency to reduce personalized and affective services to children. Some of the most obvious cases are those of the art and music experiences and often the physical and health instructional programs. Even ESL programs, which have been supported with federal funding, have been in jeopardy. These are very personal activities, touching on the emotional as much as on the intellectual personality of students. To avoid pitfalls such as these, there are things the principal, as an instructional leader, needs to be sensitive about and take into account in the exercise of leadership. There must be awareness of LEP children having unique individual personalities shaped by differences in ancestry, aspirations, backgrounds, drives, expectations, attitudes, customs, habits, and talents, to name a few. They have needs for acceptance, achievement, fulfillment, guidance, and self-respect, while at the same time they exhibit ambition, apathy, boredom, curiosity, depression, happiness, and other emotions. Instructional leaders must realize that children are combinations of many of these changes, making each of them a distinct individual. This distinct individuality changes some of its traits in the course of personal development, even from day to day, and makes it necessary to modify practices and programs to suit new needs. Principals should also know that children, because of their humanity, share many common characteristics. They share the ability to learn; they sustain patterns of growth; they are responsive to certain positive factors in the environment; and they function and conform in accordance with known and understandable natural laws.

Effective principals know that consistency in the belief that all children can learn will make education possible in every language-learning classroom. The principals' leadership is effective when the school environment is conducive to better growth, learning, and fulfillment, and when they have the best knowledge about language learners in general and LEP children in particular. In organizing ESL programs, effective principals will be mindful of a number of ideas about how learning is facilitated (Tyler, 1985). Students need stimulation, either from the environment or from within themselves, in order to learn (Cooper, 1988). Therefore, the school must provide a rich environment which appeals to the senses of all students. If students perceive the material as useful they will adapt it to their purposes; if not, they will ignore it, reject it, or tune it out (Bowles, 1968; Eisner, 1991).

Since most of the students in ESL programs come from lower socioeconomic classes, these students need to strengthen their long-term educational goals. The ESL curriculum must appear of value to them at the moment, not just as a means of preparing them for higher grades. Principals must organize the ESL program in such a way as to facilitate more successes than failures in learning tasks. In this way, they will conceive learning as being an avenue for fulfillment. When students face situations in which they perceive little likelihood of success, they refuse to become involved and divert their energies toward undesirable and unproductive behaviors. If the principal selects instructional materials above the frustration level of the students, for example, the chances of success are reduced. This is not to negate the need for presenting challenges to students. Learning takes place when there is a challenge. Challenge exists not only if the task's outcome is uncertain, but if the new tasks are similar enough to previous ones in which the students have been successful so that they may feel their chances for success are fairly high.

A principal's role is to exercise instructional leadership through proper training of teachers and to view their role as not so much to get learning accomplished but to make it seem important to the students. Principals must provide an atmosphere where human relationships are valued. They must induce on the part of ESL teachers (and other staff) a genuineness and sincerity as human beings, prizing–not just accepting–students as fellow persons with human dignity, integrity, and worth–sympathetic understanding of the students somewhere between sentimentality and cold objectivity (Boston, 1991; Sullivan, Barshay & Wogaman, 1971).

Principals' leadership founded on human values enables schools to view ESL teachers' role as selecting and arranging humanistic experiences that foster positive relationships and promote cooperation as a constant ingredient in classroom interaction. These humanistic experiences take place using language to process what is perceived, seen, heard, tasted, felt, touched, smelled, done and to relate it to other experiences stored (prior knowledge) in the memory through the miracle of the second language, and in whatever linguistic way possible, to generalize and apply to other situations not yet experienced. Through a humanistic ESL curriculum, principals can induce vicarious experiences, sharing the experiences of persons of other times and places. The curriculum should be designed to guide and encourage, more than "to teach" in order to achieve a higher order of learning.

Principals must train teachers to realize that learning a second language can cause conflicts. As they learn, students realize that the more that is learned and experienced, the more there is to know. Principals must have in place guidance support for all language learners. In experiencing and choosing what to learn, students are placed in a position where this choosing and experiencing demands considerable emotional stability if learning in depth is to occur and if it is to be consistent, continuous, and progressive. The responsibility of principals as instructional leaders is to foster a functional school organization where students can attain emotional stability and security. Limited English proficient students who, at school or at home, are subjected to emotional stresses are in no condition to learn. Finally, principals should be aware of the fact that schools cannot afford to function in isolation from the community. Collaborative efforts with other community organizations require careful planning and thoughtful use of people and places. These are essential ingredients in successful school-community collaboration and improved education for ESL and all other children and youth.

References

Boston, J. A. (1991). School leadership and global education. In K. A. Tye (Ed.), *Global education from thought to action: 1991 Yearbook of the Association for Supervision and Curriculum Development* (pp. 86-99). Alexandria, VA: Edward Brothers.

Bowles, D. R. (1968). *Effective elementary school administration.* West Nyack, NY: Parker.

Cooper, M. (1988). Whose culture is it, anyway? In A. Lieberman (Ed.), *In building a professional culture in schools* (pp. 220-226). New York: Teachers College Press.

Eisner, E. W. (1991). What really counts in schools. *Educational Leadership, 48*(5), 10-17.

Fass, P. S. (1989). *Outside in: Minorities and the transformation of American education.* New York: Oxford University Press.

Godar, J. (1990). *Teachers talk.* Macomb, IL: Glenbridge.

Hawley, R. C. & Hawley, I. L. (1975). *Human values in the classroom.* New York: Hart.

Kantrowitz, B. & Wingert, P. (1989, April 17). How kids learn. *Newsweek,* pp. 50-57.

Klopf, G. J. (1979). *The principal and staff development in the school.* New York: Bank Street College.

Knap, M. S., Trunbull, B. J. & Shields, P. M. (1990). New directions for educating the children of poverty. *Educational Leadership, 48*(1), 4-8.

Lovitt, Z. (1990). Rethinking my roots as a teacher. *Educational Leadership, 47*(6), 43-46.

Pai, Y. (1990). *Cultural foundations of education.* Columbus, OH: Merrill.

Postman, N. (1979). *Teaching as a conserving activity.* New York: Delacorte.

Sullivan, N. V., Barshay, R. & Wogaman, D. (1971). *Walk, run, or retreat: The modern school administrator.* Bloomington, IN: Indiana University Press.

Tyler, R. W. (1985). Relating school and non-school settings: Conditions for effective learning. In M. D. Fantini & R. L. Sinclair (Eds.), *Education in schools and non-school settings: Eighty-fourth yearbook of the society for the study of education* (Part I) (pp. 189-195). Chicago, IL: University of Chicago Press.

CHAPTER 12

Resources for ESL Educators

The ESL professional requires theoretical, methodological, and instructional resources in order to keep abreast with new developments in the ESL profession. A wide range of resources are available to ESL educators through many channels, including national and international service organizations, publishers, libraries, not-for-profit organizations, clearinghouses, and government agencies. This chapter presents a selective list of these resources. These resources, with the exception of the publishing companies, are grouped together since in many instances their function includes several of the sub-divisions mentioned above.

Selected Organizations

Canada Language Center
(200-549 Harve Street, Vancouver, BC V6C 2C6, Canada, 604-685-2133).

The Canada Language Center was established in 1985 to provide full-time English training to immigrants and refugees in a program sponsored by the government of Canada. The center also provides preparation for the TOEFL exam.

Center for Applied Linguistics (CAL)
(1118 22nd Street, N.W., Washington, D.C. 20037, 202-429-9292).

The Center for Applied Linguistics (CAL) was established in 1959 as an independent, not-for-profit organization which serves as a national research center dedicated to the application of findings of linguistic science to the solution of educational and social problems. CAL publishes a journal and a newsletter. The Center has been deeply involved in English language learning and teaching and possesses well-developed capabilities for assisting educators with successful instructional practices.   The center has established an extensive network of specialists who can be called upon for expertise and advice. Publications from CAL include several series on second language acquisition and applied linguistics as well as the *ERIC/CLL News Bulletin*.

Federation Internationale des Professeurs de Langues Vivant
(Seestrasse 247, CH-8038, Zurich, Switzerland, 1-482-50-40).

Promotes cooperation among language teachers of various countries; coordinates efforts and research to improve teaching methods and in-service training of teachers; stimulates exchanges, including teachers, books, and instructional materials. It organizes working groups to study particular problems; holds seminars and symposiums; advises national and international organizations on foreign language teaching reforms; and acts as liaison with government organizations and with educational, scientific, and cultural organizations.

International Association of Teachers of English as a Foreign Language
(3 Kingsdown Chambers, Kingsdown Park, Tankerton, Whitstable, Kent CT5 2DJ England, 227-276-528).

The International Association of Teachers of English as a Foreign Language (IATEFL) is a multinational, educational institution whose purpose is to exchange experience, views, and information among members of different countries so that the teaching of English might be improved at all levels and in all countries. IATEFL publishes a newsletter and a journal.

Institute of International Education
(809 United Nations Plaza, New York, N.Y. 10017, 212-984-5410).

The Institute of International Education (IIE) is the largest United States higher education exchange agency which provides information on international educational exchange.

International Reading Association
(800 Barksdale Road, P. O. Box 8139, Newark, DE 19711, 303-731-1600).

It offers a variety of publications of interest to ESL educators. These are *The Reading Teacher* for elementary school teachers, *Journal of Reading* for secondary school teachers, and *Reading Research Quarterly* for scholars and researchers.

Linguistic Society of America (LSA)
(1325 18th Street, N.W., Suite 211, Washington, D.C. 20036-6501, 202-835-1714).

The Linguistic Society of America (LSA) is a scholarly society that offers courses in theoretical and applied linguistics every two years at a host university in the United States. Publications include: *Language, LSA Bulletin, Directory of Programs in Linguistics in the U.S. and Canada,* and *Guide to Grants and Fellowships in Linguistics.*

National Association for Bilingual Education
(1201 16th Street, N.W., Room 407, Washington, D.C. 20036, 202-822-7870).

The National Association for Bilingual Education (NABE) was founded in 1975 as an advocacy force to address the educational needs of the linguistic minority populations of the United States. NABE annual conferences stimulate an exchange of ideas among those involved in bilingual education and English as a second language. Educators benefit from NABE through conferences, pedagogical practices in bilingual education, pedagogical practices in teaching English as a second language, and educational reform for linguistic minority students. NABE publishes *The Journal of the National Association for Bilingual Education* and the *NABE News*.

National Clearinghouse for Bilingual Education
(1118 22nd Street, N.W., Washington, D.C. 20037, 800-321-NCBE).

The National Clearinghouse for Bilingual Education (NCBE) has been operating since 1977. NCBE is funded by the United States Department of Education, Office of Bilingual Education and Minority Language Affairs (OBEMLA) for the purpose of providing practitioners with information on the education of limited English proficient students. NCBE coordinates, and addresses with a network of federally supported projects, the needs of educators in instructing language minority students.

National Council of Teachers of English
(1111 Kenyon Road, Urbana, IL).

The NCTE offers a variety of professional resources on the teaching of English and the Language Arts in addition to publishing professional journals for teachers. These include *Language Arts*, for elementary school teachers, *English Journal*, for secondary teachers, and *Research in the Teaching of English* for scholars and researchers.

Teachers of English to Speakers of Other Languages
(1600 Cameron St., Suite 300, Alexandria, VA 22314-2751, 703-836-0774).

The Association of Teachers of English to Speakers of other Languages (TESOL) was established in 1966. It is concerned with the teaching of English as a second or foreign language. TESOL was created with the purpose of bringing together ESL teachers and administrators at all educational levels. TESOL membership includes a newsletter, the *TESOL Matters*, the *TESOL Quarterly*, *TESOL Journal*, and access to a job-bank file, plus a variety of other services and opportunities such as reduced rates at the annual convention and the summer institute. TESOL also publishes and distributes a wide range of professional resource materials, which are available to members at reduced rates.

The Foundation Center

(79 Fifth Avenue, New York, N.Y. 10003, 212-620-4230).

The Foundation Center provides the general public with comprehensive information on foundation and corporation grant sources. Services, including orientation and educational seminars, are offered free of charge. The Foundation Center also offers free access to its resources and services.

Office of Bilingual Education and Minority Languages Affairs (OBEMLA)

(U.S. Department of Education, 400 Maryland Avenue, Room 5628, Washington, D.C. 202-732-1843).

The Office of Bilingual Education and Minority Language Affairs (OBEMLA) is part of the United States Department of Education, which administers all Title VII funds. OBEMLA provides grants to school districts to facilitate in children the acquisition of English. It also provides bilingual education training grants, support services, bilingual vocational training, and research on language minority students. All these grants provide opportunities through several means for students to become proficient in English.

Directory of Language Related Organizations

Administrators and Teachers
of English as a Second
Language
1860 19th Street, N.W.
Washington, D.C. 22019

American Council for the
Teaching of Foreign
Languages (ACTFL)
ACTFL, 6 Executive Plaza
Yonkers, N.Y. 10701-6801

Australian Federation of the
Modern Language Teachers
Association (AFMLTA)
P.O. Box 42446
Casuarina, Northern Territory
Australia

British Association of Applied
Linguistics (BAAL)
University of Reading
P.O. Box 218 Whiternights
Reading RG6 England

Canadian Association of
Second Language Teachers
(CASLT)
CASLT, 369 Montrose St.
Winnipeg, Manitoba
R3M 3M1, Canada

Canadian Linguistic
Association (CLA)
CIL 92, Department de
Langues et linguistique,
Universite Level
Quebec, Canada

Children's Book Council
67 Irving Place
New York, N.Y. 10003

Council for Exceptional
Children (CEC) and the
Division for Culturally and
Linguistically Diverse
Exceptional Learners (DDEL)
1920 Association Dr.
Reston, Virginia 22091-1589

Council on Interracial Books
for Children, Inc.
1841 Broadway
New York, N.Y. 10023

Consulate of Spain
Education Office
1500 Fifth Avenue, Suite 918
New York, N.Y. 10011

Children's Book Press
1461 Ninth Avenue
San Francisco, CA. 94122

Children's Defense Fund
(CDF)
122 C Street N.W.
Washington, D.C. 20001

English Academy of Southern
Africa Language Education
Centre, School of Education
University of Cape Town
Private Bag
Rondebosch 7700
South Africa

English Language Institute
P.O. Box 4452,
1640 Kalima Rd., N.W.
Washington, D.C. 20012

English Teacher Association
of Israel (ETAI)
Hebrew University of
Jerusalem, ETAI, POB 7663
Jerusalem, Israel 91076

English Teachers Association
Switzerland (ETAS)
Lausanne, Switzerland

ERIC Clearinghouse on
Languages and Linguistics
1118 22nd Street, NW
Washington, D.C. 20037

Federation Internationale des
Professeurs de Langues
Vivantes (FIPLV)
Via Bruzzesi 39, I-20146
Milano, Italy

Good Apple
Box 299
Carthage, Illinois 62321

Great Book Foundation
40 East Huron Street
Chicago, Illinois 60611

International Association of
Applied Linguistics (AILA)
Vrije Universiteit
Faculteit der Letteren
Postbus 7161, NL-1007 MC
Amsterdam, The Netherlands

International Association of
Teachers of English as a
Foreign Language (IATEFL)
IATEFL-Hungary
Ajtosi Durer sor 19-21,
Budapest 1146, Hungary

International Association of
Teachers of English as a
Foreign Language (IATEFL)
3 Kingsdown Chambers,
Kingsdown Park, Tankerton,
Whitstable, Kent
CT5 2Dj, England

International Society for
Intercultural Education,
Training, and Research
(SIETAR)
733 15th St., N.W., Suite 900
Washington, D.C. 20005

La Casa de la Herencia
Puertorriqueña
1 East 104th Street, Suite 458,
New York, N.Y. 10029

Linguistic Association of
Canada and the US (LACUS)
P.O. Box 101
Lake Bluff, Illinois 60044

Linguistic Society of America
(LSA)
1325 18th St., N.W.,
Washington, D.C. 20036-6501

Literacy Assistance Center
15 Dutch Street, 4th Floor,
New York, N.Y. 10003

Modern Language Association
(MLA)
10 Astor Place
New York, N.Y. 10003-6981

Museo del Barrio
1230 Fifth Avenue
New York, N.Y. 10029

National Association of
Foreign Students Affairs:
Association of International
Educators (NAFSA: AIE)
1875 Connecticut Ave., N.W.
Suite 1000
Washington, D.C. 20009

National Council of Teachers
of English (NCTE)
1111 Kenyon Rd.
Urbana, Ill 61801

New York Association for
Bilingual Education (SABE)
Fordham University at Lincoln
Center, Room 1025, New
York, N.Y. 10023

Regional English Language
Centre (RELC)
SEAMEO Regional Language
Centre
30 Orange Grove Rd.
Singapore 1025,
Republic of Singapore

Society for Accelerative
Learning and Teaching
(SALT)
3028 Emerson Ave., S.,
Minneapolis, MN 55408

South African Applied
Linguistics Association
(SAALA)
Language Education Centre
School of Education

University of Cape Town
Private Bag
Rondebosch 7700
South Africa

Southwest Conference on
Language Teaching
(SWCOLT)
10724 Tancred
Northglenn, Colorado 80234

Teachers Networking
P.O. Box 819
New York, N.Y. 10085

The Bilingual Resource
Library
New York City Public Schools
131 Livingston Street
Room 204
Brooklyn, N.Y. 11201

The Caribbean Cultural Center
408 West 58th Street
New York, N.Y. 10019

Washington Association of
Foreign Language Teachers
(WAFLT)
15341 S.E. 182nd St.
Renton, Washington 98058

AUTHOR INDEX

SUBJECT INDEX

Age, 41-45
Aptitude, 34-35
Assessment, 71-72, 170-172
Attitude, 36-38

Bilingual education, 111-114
    transitional, 114
    developmental, 112-113
    two-way, 113-114
    special alternative, 114

Cognitive model, 8-9
Cognive style, 38-39
College ESL, 105-106
Communicative approach, 27
Community, 59-60
Content based, 123-124
Contrastive analysis, 22-23
Counseling learning approach, 122
Culture, 53-61

Discourse analysis, 24

Eclectic approach, 125-126
Elementary school, 93-94
Emotionally disturbed, 175
English proficiency, 78-81
English for specific purposes, 105
Error analysis, 23

SOURCE BOOKS ON EDUCATION

BILINGUAL EDUCATION
A Source Book for Educators
by Alba N. Ambert and Sarah Melendez

TEACHING SCIENCE TO YOUNG CHILDREN
A Resource Book
by Mary D. Iatridis

SPECIAL EDUCATION
A Source Book
by Manny Sternlicht

COMPUTERS IN THE CLASS-ROOM . . . WHAT SHALL I DO?
A Guide
by Walter Burke

SCHOOL PLAY
A Source Book
by James H. Block and Nancy R. King

COMPUTER SIMULATIONS
A Source Book to Learning in an Electronic Environment
by Jerry Willis, Larry Hovey, and Kathleen Hovey

PROJECT HEAD START
Past, Present, and Future Trends in the Context of Family Needs
by Valora Washington and Ura Jean Oyemade

ADULT LITERACY
A Source Book and Guide
by Joyce French

MATHEMATICS EDUCATION IN SECONDARY SCHOOLS AND TWO-YEAR COLLEGES
A Source Book
by Louise S. Grinstein and Paul J. Campbell

BLACK CHILDREN AND AMERICAN INSTITUTIONS
An Ecological Review and Resource Guide
by Valora Washington and Velma LaPoint

SEXUALITY EDUCATION
A Resource Book
by Carol Cassell and Pamela M. Wilson

REFORMING TEACHER EDUCATION
Issues and New Directions
edited by Joseph A. Braun, Jr.

EDUCATIONAL TECHNOLOGY
Planning and Resource Guide Supporting Curriculum
by James E. Eisele and Mary Ellin Eisele

CRITICAL ISSUES IN FOREIGN LANGUAGE INSTRUCTION
edited by Ellen S. Silber

THE EDUCATION OF WOMEN IN THE UNITED STATES
A Guide to Theory, Teaching, and Research
by Averil Evans McClelland

MATERIALS AND STRATEGIES FOR THE EDUCATION OF TRAINABLE MENTALLY RETARDED LEARNERS
by James P. White

RURAL EDUCATION
Issues and Practice
by Alan J. DeYoung

EDUCATIONAL TESTING
Issues and Applications
by Kathy E. Green

THE WRITING CENTER
New Directions
edited by Ray Wallace and Jeanne Simpson

TEACHING THINKING SKILLS
Theory and Practice
by Joyce N. French and Carol Rhoder

TEACHING SOCIAL STUDIES TO THE YOUNG CHILD
A Research and Resource Guide
by Blythe S. Farb Hinitz

TELECOMMUNICATIONS
A Handbook for Educators
by Reza Azarmsa

CATHOLIC SCHOOL EDUCATION IN THE UNITED STATES
Development and Current Concerns
by Mary A. Grant and Thomas C. Hunt

DAY CARE
A Source Book
Second Edition, by Kathleen Pullan Watki and Lucius Durant, Jr.

SCHOOL PRINCIPALS AND CHANGE
by Michael D. Richardson, Paula M. Short, and Robert L. Prickett

PLAY IN PRACTICE
A Systems Approach to Making Good Play Happen
edited by Karen VanderVen,
Paul Niemiec, and Roberta Schomburg

TEACHING SCIENCE TO CHILDREN
Second Edition
by Mary D. Iatridis with a contribution by
Miriam Maracek

**KITS, GAMES AND MANIPULATIVES
FOR THE ELEMENTARY SCHOOL
CLASSROOM**
A Source Book
by Andrea Hoffman and Ann Glannon

PARENTS AND SCHOOLS
A Source Book
by Angela Carrasquillo
and Clement B. G. London

PROJECT HEAD START
Models and Strategies for the Twenty-First Century
by Valora Washington
and Ura Jean Oyemade Bailey

**INSTRUMENTATION
IN EDUCATION**
An Anthology
by Lloyd Bishop and Paula E. Lester

**TEACHING ENGLISH
AS A SECOND LANGUAGE**
A Resource Guide
by Angela L. Carrasquillo